APOSTASY IN ISLAM

A Historical and Scriptural Analysis

APOSTASY IN ISLAM

A Historical and Scriptural Analysis

TAHA JABIR ALALWANI

Based on the original Arabic translated by
Nancy Roberts

THE INTERNATIONAL INSTITUTE OF ISLAMIC THOUGHT
LONDON · WASHINGTON

THE INTERNATIONAL INSTITUTE OF ISLAMIC THOUGHT
P.O. BOX 669, HERNDON, VA 20172, USA
WWW.IIIT.ORG

LONDON OFFICE
P.O. BOX 126, RICHMOND, SURREY TW9 2UD, UK
WWW.IIITUK.COM

ISBN 978-1-56564-363-5 paperback
ISBN 978-1-56564-364-2 hardback

Typesetting and Cover Design by Shiraz Khan
Printed in Malta by Gutenberg Press Ltd

CONTENTS

FOREWORD

Of knowledge, we have none, save what
You have taught us. (The Qur'an 2:32)

THE INTERNATIONAL INSTITUTE OF ISLAMIC THOUGHT (IIIT) presents this scholarly work on the topic of *al-riddah* (apostasy in Islam) to cast new light on the issue. The author Taha J. Alalwani is an internationally known scholar and expert in the fields of Islamic legal theory, jurisprudence (fiqh), and *uṣūl al-fiqh*.

The subject of apostasy is arguably one of the most controversial to have afflicted the Muslim world throughout its history. What is the legally prescribed penalty, if any, for apostasy, and how does this relate to the demand for religious tolerance as stipulated in verse 2:256 of the Qur'an "There shall be no compulsion in matters of faith"? As the historical debate between Muslim scholars drags on, so the controversy drags on, with Islamic jurisprudence being accused of a flagrant disregard for human rights and freedom of expression. Apostasy continues to be the focus of much damaging media coverage today.

The book examines debates surrounding the issue in careful detail. Disputing arguments put forward by proponents of the death penalty, the author contends that evidence from the Qur'an and the Sunnah does not support the implementation of a capital punishment for the sin of *al-riddah*. Rather, textual study points to freedom of belief including the act of rejecting the faith. Furthermore, it is only within a specific and politically charged, particularly in terms of national security, context that the question of a penalty arises, because at this point the act of apostasy becomes a crime in addition to being a sin.

As well as rigorously examining the Qur'an and the Sunnah, the author also investigates the standpoint of the various juristic schools of thought, analyzing their views on apostasy and the evidence cited in support of punishment; important because those Muslim jurists who have claimed that the apostate should be put to death have done so based not only on their own understanding of the verbal Sunnah of the Prophet (ṢAAS)§ but also on "scholastic consensus". The author makes clear that there has in fact been no such consensus concerning the existence of a legally prescribed punishment, set down in the Qur'an and clarified in the Sunnah, for apostasy in the sense in which we are using this term today. What becomes quickly apparent is that analysis and debate have become confused with the idea of a politicised exit, such that the nature of the crime which jurists often cite is in fact not the one we are solely concerned with – one of the pure sin of apostasy or the rejection of Islam after having accepted it. In fact their discussions primarily centre around a compound crime involving political, legal and social elements, such that an apostate's change of religion or religious belief has adverse affects on his/her actions toward the security and well being of Muslim society and the systems and laws under which it operates. Likewise, the author does not advocate allowing the apostate to gather about him/herself a community of like-minded people striving to effect damaging change to the tenets and principles of the Islamic faith, that is within the Muslim society. The whole issue then becomes one of context, such that when apostasy threatens harm to the Muslim community and/or plots to destabilize society, it then moves into the realms of an offence akin to treason, and subject to capital punishment.

Islam teaches that human beings possess the freedom to choose the religion by which they wish to worship God. It is a freedom which, the author emphasizes, Allah (SWT)§§ has entrusted us with, and which serves as the basis for human responsibility; and it is a choice which will be judged in the hereafter, not in this life. One of the most interesting aspects to which he points as evidence that punishment for the sin of apostasy (in the afterlife) rests with God is that of repetition:

---

§ (ṢAAS) – *Ṣallā Allāhu ʿalayhi wa sallam.* May the peace and blessings of God be upon him. Said whenever the name of Prophet Muhammad is mentioned.

§§ (SWT) – *Subḥānahu wa Taʿālā*: May He be praised and may His transcendence be affirmed. Said when referring to God.

> Behold, as for those who come to believe, and then deny the truth, and again come to believe, and again deny the truth, and thereafter grow stubborn in their denial of the truth – God will not forgive them, nor will He guide them in any way. (4:137)

A study of this kind requires a clear methodology and a strong analytical, evidence-based approach. The author takes into consideration traditional approaches to the study of the Islamic textual sciences and other fields of knowledge, giving primary importance to the Qur'an, followed by the Sunnah, the actions of the *Ṣaḥābah*, and finally scholastic interpretation.

It is hoped that this work widens discourse, stimulate debates, and hopefully paves the way for further research. Doubtless readers may agree with some of the issues raised, and disagree with others, but it is hoped that overall they will benefit from the issues explored and the perspectives offered.

Where dates are cited according to the Islamic calendar (hijrah) they are labelled AH. Otherwise they follow the Gregorian calendar and labelled CE where necessary. Arabic words are italicized except for those which have entered common usage. Diacritical marks have been added only to those Arabic names not considered contemporary.

The IIIT, established in 1981, has served as a major center to facilitate serious scholarly efforts based on Islamic vision, values and principles. The Institute's programs of research, seminars and conferences during the last thirty years have resulted in the publication of more than four hundred titles both in English, Arabic and other major languages.

We would like to express our thanks to the translator Nancy Roberts for the quality of her work, as well as to the editorial and production team at the IIIT London Office. They include Shiraz Khan, Dr. Maryam Mahmood and Tahira Hadi. Special thanks go to Dr. Iqbal Unus for his critical reading and careful abridgment of the original manuscript. Dr. Unus' guiding hand proved invaluable in producing a clearly focused and condensed text for which he takes full credit.

IIIT LONDON OFFICE
August 2011

INTRODUCTION

This present study is based on a more extensive study on this important subject and includes two discussions of particular importance. One of these is a chapter which deals with the words spoken by the Prophet as transmitted to us in relevant Prophetic hadiths and traditions*[1] attributed to his Companions. This discussion serves as a follow-up to the preceding chapter about apostasy in the practice-based Sunnah, that is, in the Prophet's actions. In this way, all of the evidence taken together serves to evaluate if there is or there is not a clearly specified, legally prescribed punishment in Islam for the crime of altering one's religious beliefs so long as no other criminal action is associated with it.

One section of the book is devoted to a discussion of the various juristic schools of thought, particularly in view of the fact that the majority of Muslim jurists have based their claim that the apostate must be put to death on the verbal Sunnah and consensus. For this reason, it is necessary to examine these schools of thought one by one and gain a detailed familiarity with their claims, as well as the evidence on which such claims are based. Upon closer examination, it became apparent that the crime with which these jurists were dealing was not the one with which we are concerned here. That is to say, they were discussing a compound crime which involved political, legal and social elements such that an apostate's change of religion or religious belief was the outcome of a change in his attitude toward the Muslim community, and hence, toward the society, the political leadership, and the systems and laws which the community had adopted. In short, it was the result of a complete change of affiliation and loyalty.

In discussing the claim to a consensus concerning the necessity of putting the apostate to death, this study aims to make clear that there has, in fact, been no consensus concerning the existence of a legally prescribed punishment, set down in the Qur'an and clarified in the Sunnah, for apostasy in the sense in which this term is being used. Rather, in Islam, human beings possess the freedom to choose the religion by means of which they will worship God. It is a freedom with which God Almighty has entrusted us, and it is this freedom which serves as the basis for human responsibility. After all, someone who has no choice is outside the realm of accountability and bears no responsibility for what he or she does. To the extent that one's freedom of choice is diminished, one's responsibility is likewise diminished. Hence, everything that God has enjoined upon human beings or forbidden to them, He has bound to their God-given abilities, potentials and freedom of choice: "God does not burden any human being with more than He has given him – [and it may be that] God will grant, after hardship, ease" (65:7).

God Almighty has thus made what human beings seek subject to their free wills:

> And say, "The truth [has now come] from your Sustainer; let, then, him who wills, believe in it, and let him who wills, reject it." Verily, for all who sin against themselves [by rejecting Our truth] We have readied a fire whose billowing folds will encompass them from all sides; and if they beg for water, they will be given water [hot] like molten lead, which will scald their faces; how dreadful a drink, and how evil a place to rest! (18:29)

As such, He has made the human will fully effective in the realm of choice:

> Unto him who cares for [no more than the enjoyment of] this fleeting life, We readily grant thereof as much as We please, [giving] to whomever it is Our will [to give]; but in the end We consign him to

> [the suffering of] hell, which he will have to endure disgraced and disowned! But as for those who care for the [good of the] life to come, and strive for it as it ought to be striven for and are [true] believers withal – they are the ones whose striving finds favor [with God]! (17:18–19)

In the realm of human responsibility, God Almighty has made a distinction between the punishment merited by an error and that which is merited for a deliberate act, just as He draws a distinction between an error resulting from negligence and one that results from a conscious intention, and between persisting in an error and continuing to commit it, and turning away from it and repenting of it. All these things, among others, confirm the freedom enjoyed by human beings with respect to their wills, intentions, thoughts, expressions and actions. This will become increasingly clear in the course of this study, which is presented here as an example of the type of serious review needed in order to purify our heritage of the accretions with which it has become burdened over the course of certain historical periods and due to a variety of causes.

METHODOLOGY

The methodology most appropriate to this study is one which combines the conventional philosophical approach, the analytical approach, and the inductive, historical approach, yet without disregarding the traditional approaches to the study of Islamic textual sciences and other fields of knowledge which have been adhered to since the era in which the Islamic sciences first began to be recorded.

In the realm of Qur'anic interpretation, this study relies on what has been established by Muslim scholars who specialize in this field based on its particular principles and methods. Similarly, in weighing and judging hadiths, it adheres to the methods used by hadith scholars. In the realm of basic principles and foundations, it deals with the Qur'an as the foundational source for all rulings: "Judgment rests with God alone" (12:40). In other words, the principle of the authority of Scripture is considered paramount. The

Sunnah it is treated as the source which clarifies the meaning of the Qur'an in a binding manner. At the same time, claims to the existence of a consensus on matters concerning which it has been established that there was disagreement among the Companions are not accepted. After all, 'consensus' is the consensus of the Companions.

In seeking to determine the meanings of linguistic terms which appear in the Qur'an, the first criterion will be the Qur'an's own usage of such terms. The second criterion will be the Prophet's explanatory statements in the Sunnah, and the third will be the Arabs' customary usage of such terms in their various dialects, literary styles and rhetoric. By following this order of priority, one ensures that Arabs' linguistic usages of terms are not allowed to determine the meanings of the Qur'an. More broadly speaking, this study observes the governing values and intents of Islamic law in their capacity as universals, that is, as sources of light by which the path is illumined for those seeking the truth in their attempts to determine the meanings of particular texts.

THE STUDY'S LIMITATIONS AND FUNDAMENTAL PURPOSE

When jurists engage in the practice of independent interpretation, or ijtihad,* they generally begin by extracting (a) the basis of the legal ruling to be determined, (b) isolating or distinguishing this basis from other possible bases, and then (c) verifying this basis (*taḥqīq al-manāṭ*). When the issue of concern is one around which controversy or disagreement exists such that there are relevant texts from the Islamic written corpus which appear to be contradictory or in opposition to one another, such scholars begin by "clearing the playing field", as it were, that is, by clarifying what their purposes are, and what they are not.

The fundamental issue addressed in this study is individual apostasy, that is to say, a change in an individual's doctrinal beliefs and whatever modification to which this change leads in thought, conceptions and behavior. In such a case, the individual concerned has not associated the act of changing his doctrinal beliefs with rebellion against the community or its statutes, nor against its legitimate leadership, whether political or religious. He has not engaged in highway robbery or taken up arms against the community; nor has he joined the community's enemies or betrayed the community in any way. All he has done is to change his doctrinal position as a result of uncertainties and factors which have led him to doubt the community's overall doctrine or some of its pillars or foundations. Unable to resist such doubts and suspicions, he has succumbed to them and allowed them to influence him. Yet rather than becoming a public advocate of his newly adopted position, he has kept his apostasy to himself.

Granting that such an individual has indeed committed apostasy and denied the truth of Islam, the question is: Has God established death as the legally sanctioned punishment for such a person, with or without the community's first having urged him to repent? And is it, therefore, the duty of the Muslim community, represented by its rulers, to carry out this penalty by putting him to death for no reason but that he has changed his beliefs? And is this the case even if the change in this person's beliefs has not been accompanied by any other crime such as those we have mentioned? If some member of the Muslim community were to kill this individual, would he be exempt from punishment or retaliation for anything other than having taken the law into his own hands? Similarly, is it the Muslim community's duty to compel this person and others like him to return to Islam by force? Or does the Qur'an deny the legitimacy of such compulsion? Further: Has there been unanimous agreement since the dawn of Islam that it is the Muslim community's duty to put the apostate to death? Or has this view been the subject of disagreement that has not been brought sufficiently to light?

If one accepts the view that the apostate must be put to death, does this mean that the mere denial of Islam is sufficient legal cause for carrying out the death penalty? In other words, is apostasy to be viewed as a mere departure from Islam, or as an act of aggression against it? Do the majority of those who support the death penalty for apostasy view it as a political crime, or as belonging to the category of felonies, in which case its punishment will take on the character of a legally prescribed penalty? Moreover, assuming that it is a legally prescribed penalty and that, as is stated explicitly in authoritative Islamic texts, the legally prescribed penalties serve to atone for a person's sin, then is the death penalty for apostasy to be considered a form of purification or atonement?

These are the basic questions addressed in this study. In so doing, this study adheres to the methodology outlined above, asking the Most High for guidance to the most truthful point of view, for it is He alone who grants success.

The aim of this study is to provide a model for the type of revision by means of which one can place Islamic tradition under the authority of the Qur'an, thereby bringing it into full conformity with Qur'anic teachings.

I

IS APOSTASY A CAPITAL CRIME?

The majority of Muslim scholars have closed the door to discussion of this question with the sword of 'consensus'. The claim to such a consensus was adopted long ago as a means of preventing the review of certain critical issues, such as this one, despite the existence of disagreement over the Islamic legal ruling on apostasy (*al-riddah*) during the first three centuries after the dawn of Islam. Yet despite this lack of consensus during the early days of Islam, those who maintain the existence of a legally prescribed death penalty for apostasy in Islamic law have claimed that such a consensus existed. Is so doing, they have sought to divert attention from the fact that ʿUmar ibn al-Khaṭṭāb, Ibrāhīm al-Nakhʿī, Sufyān al-Thawrī and others did not support such a penalty. In this way they have sought to forestall any rethinking of this penalty on the part of later thinkers. After all, who would dare to reconsider a legal ruling on which all the scholars of the entire Ummah are in agreement?

Is apostasy to be classified as an expression of one's personal opinion, or as an act of aggression against the community and its collective rights? Is there really a consensus on the necessity of killing someone who apostatizes from Islam? In dealing with acts of apostasy, should priority be given to the individual's right to express his personal views and beliefs, or to the community's right to preserve and protect those things it holds most sacred?

APOSTASY IN THE NEWS

In the year 2006, the eyes of the entire world were riveted on a case of open apostasy involving an Afghani citizen by the name of Abd al-Rahman Abd al-Mannan. After going to work for a Christian relief agency operating in the city of Peshawar, Pakistan in 1990, this man had been influenced by his coworkers to become a Christian. In 1993 Abd al-Rahman traveled to Germany in an unsuccessful attempt to obtain political asylum there. He then sought political asylum in Belgium, again without success, after which he returned to Afghanistan in 2002. During this period of time, his Muslim wife had asked for a divorce due to his conversion, which was her undisputed right, and her request was granted.

Abd al-Rahman did not deny his conversion, and there ensued disputes between both he and his former wife over custody of their daughters, with the wife claiming that Abd al-Rahman was incompetent to raise them for fear that he might convert them to Christianity. A number of evangelistic tracts and books, in addition to copies of the New Testament, were found in his house, and in February, 2006, protracted litigations between him and his wife ended with his being imprisoned. No sooner had he been incarcerated than the world media transformed him into a long-awaited saint who was about to be martyred for Christ. This was followed by intervention by US President George Bush, Secretary of State Condoleezza Rice, Italian Prime Minister Silvio Berlesconi and others, who pressured Afghani President Hamid Karzai to release him and send him to safety in Italy, where rightist Berlesconi was facing the most important electoral challenge in his political career against the leftist alliance. Karzai pressured the court to release Abd al-Rahman on the pretext that he was mentally deranged and not fit to stand trial for his actions. He was released on March 27, 2006 and arrived in Italy on March 29, where Berlesconi granted him political asylum, thereby to appear before his voters as the protector of liberty, humanity and the holy cross.[1]

CONSTANTS AND VARIABLES

Every nation on earth has a set of constants or unchanging values which it is careful to preserve and which it attempts to hedge about with a wall of guarantees and protections lest they be violated, altered, distorted, mocked or ridiculed. Perhaps the most important shared value that all nations acknowledge as a constant and which they do their utmost to protect is that of national identity. The identity of a nation is its very being, and as such, it is something it can never relinquish, and concerning no aspect or component of which it can be tolerant or lax. The identities of nations may differ in their elements and components. Hence, what one nation views as part of its identity may not be viewed thus by another nation. However, that which every nation shares in common with all other nations is the necessity of respecting that nation's identity and preserving it with all its component elements. It follows, then, that every nation sees it as its duty to spare nothing, however precious, for the sake of preserving its identity with all that goes to make it up.

Prior to the age in which we live, nearly every nation considered its religion to be the most vital component element of its identity. This included even pagan nations such as the Roman Empire both before and after the adoption of Christianity,[2] the Babylonians, and other civilizations and nations, particularly those whose existence, structure and identity were tied up with their having adopted and identified themselves with a specific religion.[3] This being the case, Muslim scholars were not far from the mark when they counted religion among the five essential human needs, viewing it as the basis for numerous important rulings in Islamic law; foremost among such rulings was that concerning jihad, which is viewed as a means of defending and protecting the Islamic religion on the national level.

The legally prescribed punishment for apostasy, according to some, applies on both the individual and collective levels, since it is said to be based on the need to protect the religion from those who would seek to do it harm, manipulate it, or rebel against it. In issuing rulings to this effect, Muslim scholars have perceived no contradiction between the unanimously recognized principle of religious freedom as enshrined in the Qur'an's declaration that "There shall be no coercion in matters of faith," and their affirmation of a death penalty for apostasy. Through the various periods of our Islamic history, this affirmation has constituted the prevailing point of view. Consequently, the views of prominent early scholars who disagreed with the overwhelming majority – including individuals of weight and influence the likes of the Companion ʿUmar ibn al-Khaṭṭāb (martyred in the year 23 AH/644 CE), Ibrāhīm al-Nakhʿī (d. 196 AH/811 CE), and Sufyān al-Thawrī (d. 161 AH/777 CE), as well as other illustrious figures – did not receive publicity or wide circulation. Given this fact, it was easy for the transmitters of Islamic jurisprudence to promote the claim that there was a 'consensus' concerning the ruling which had been adopted by the majority of fiqh scholars, namely, that the apostate must be compelled to return to Islam on pain of death. The perceived purpose behind this ruling was to protect the religion from attempts to undervalue it or to undermine its function as the foundation on the basis of which the Muslim nation came into being, the foundation of the state's legitimacy, and the source of Islamic doctrine, law, and all related life systems within the Muslim state. It comes as no surprise, then, that this ruling has come to be widely accepted as one of the unchanging, agreed-upon legally prescribed punishments, and that as a consequence, the thought of discussing it has been rejected out of hand by many. After all, how can one open up for reconsideration something that has been the subject of unanimous agreement among Muslim scholars?

Were it not for the challenges of contemporary civilization, which has opened up virtually everything to critique, revision and analysis, no conversation would ever have opened up on this topic. Given the fact that this ruling conflicts with the human right to choose the doctrine in which one will believe and the religion one will profess, and to express one's beliefs freely without compulsion, a discussion of it was originally opened by reformers Jamal al-Din al-Afghani, Muhammad Abduh, Rashid Rida[4] and others. These reformers had become aware of the concern of who said: Since Islam teaches the necessity of forcing an apostate to return to Islam on pain of death, this means there is compulsion in Islam and a disregard for the freedom of belief and expression. The reformers' responses to this concern were varied. Al-Afghani wrote his famous book, *Al-Radd ʿalā al-Ḍahriyyīn* as an affirmation of the need for Muslims to obey the Qur'anic injunction to debate peaceably with those who disagree with them, respond to their claims, and confute the doubts or arguments they raise with Islamic proofs and evidence.

However, the matter was not settled at that time. On the contrary, it remained a matter of controversy over which tempers flared whenever anyone raised it anew or even made reference to it. Some contemporary scholars spoke in a whisper of points of view that went against the prevailing perspective, according to which the death penalty for apostasy was a matter of consensus. Such scholars also expressed their doubts concerning the evidence others had cited in support of the prevailing view as a means of making the issue appear to be settled and no longer open to discussion. It was reported, for example, that Shaltut (d. 1963 CE) was among the skeptics, followed by Muhammad Abu Zahrah (d. 1974 CE) and others.[5] However, these scholars did not go public with their point of view. Rather, they chose to remain silent, or to content themselves with speaking in a whisper and repeating what their forebears had said before them, namely, "I know things which, were I to speak of them, such-and-such and such-and-such would be my lot ..." Thus it was that the file remained open, yet closed. This phase was followed in 1985 by the execution of Mahmud Muhammad Taha in the Sudan when Jafar Numayri, president of the Sudan at that time, announced the enforcement of the rulings laid down in Islamic law. At that time, Dr. Hasan al-Turabi – who holds a point of view on the legally prescribed punishment for apostasy which is well-known among his students, supporters and close associates, but which he had not declared publicly at that time – was the Sudan's public prosecutor. The Sudanese court, headed at that time by Judge al-Kabbāshī, issued a verdict condemning the 79-year-old man to death, and the execution was carried out without any objections being raised.

When Faysal ibn Musaid murdered his paternal uncle, King Faysal in 1974, he was sentenced to death by the sword "as the penalty for apostasy." The man had confessed to the crime of premeditated murder, which was sufficient in and of itself to justify his execution. Hence, scholars and judges connected to the case had no need to cite any other crime on the basis of which to put him to death; even so, mention was made of his apostasy as being among the legal reasons on which the verdict had been based. At that time there was not much debate over the issue of his apostasy and whether it was to be considered the principle crime, or a secondary crime to that of murder. Apparently, no mention of this question was made in the court's verdict.

This was followed by the Salman Rushdie affair, the resulting debate, and the various fatwas that were issued in this connection, including the famed fatwa handed down by Imam Khomeini (d. 1989) declaring it lawful to take Rushdie's life. This case entered the international spotlight, and talk circulated in the West about how human rights are not respected in Islam and among Muslims, including the right to free expression and to the choice of religious belief and profession. In short, Islam was declared hostile to the highest of all values in the contemporary West, namely, freedom.[6] Many of the fatwas and books that came out in this connection were reminiscent of the positions that had been taken by Muslim jurists in the past, and the arguments and evidence they had cited in support of the claim that according to Islamic law, the apostate must be put to death.

Then came the case surrounding the murder of Farag Fawdah at the hands of a number of youths belonging to Islamic groups in Egypt. Their lawyer summoned Egypt's most moderate shaykh at that time, namely, Muhammad al-Ghazali, may he rest in peace (d. 1996), who felt himself obliged to confirm the teachings of the prevailing schools of Islamic jurisprudence on this matter, namely, the necessity of putting the apostate to death. Declaring Farag Fawdah an apostate who had deserved death, al-Ghazali maintained that all these youths had done was to carry out Islamic law as it applies to someone who may be killed with impunity, and whose blood is no longer sacred nor of any value. The state, he said, should have killed him itself, or by means of its organs, and since it had failed to do so, these youths had taken the law into their own hands and carried out the penalty that the state should have carried out itself.

Al-Ghazali's statements sparked a huge uproar in Egypt. Heated discussions ensued between Muslim scholars, lawyers, human rights activists, journalists and other liberals, and the issue produced an unprecedented split in Egypt's educated elite. The documents that were published and circulated in the course of discussing the issue in the press came to approximately nine large volumes. Yet the door was not closed, and the debate was not resolved. Then, hardly had the dust on this case settled when another, similar, case emerged, namely, that of Dr. Nasr Hamid Abu Zayd. Dr. Abu Zayd had been accused of apostasy and someone had brought suit against him, claiming that he should be separated from his wife and treated as an apostate. The file was thus opened once again, with people exchanging arguments and counter-arguments until the documents published in connection with the ensuing debate had swelled to around five large volumes. Add to these the books written by the accused himself, the most important of which is *Al-Tafkīr fī Zamān al-Takfīr* (Thought in the Age of Charging Others With Unbelief), not to mention his radio interviews and television debates. Inundated with offers of teaching posts in European and Western universities, Dr. Abu Zayd was thus transformed into another of freedom's symbols, and he and Muhammad Arkoun became consultants for a major Western encyclopedic work, overseen by the University of Leiden, dealing with the Qur'an.

Before the ink had dried on Abu Zayd's case, still another case was opened, this one related to one Dr. Hasan Hanafi, who faced the same accusation. However, it appears that Azhar University and some other institutions thought it wise to contain the furor this time. Hence, not long after the attack was made on Dr. Hasan, he was granted the honor of declaring his allegiance to Islam. Yet even after this, the United Nations, its satellite institutions, and other organs of the new world order continued launching offensives on Islam. They claimed, for example, that Islam is one of the most hostile religions in the world to freedom and human rights, as evidenced by the fact that it has continued to cling to the notion of apostasy as a crime punishable by death.

How, then, one may ask, can Muslims deal with this difficulty which continues to plague them, and which has become a means of alienating people from Islam and bringing it under attack? In 2002, Egypt's attention was focused on the case of Nawal al-Sadawi and the suit that was brought against her demanding that she be separated from her husband after she had made statements which were published in a certain magazine and in which she spoke somewhat derisively of certain juristic rulings. In this connection, one may note two public stances taken by Dr. Nawal al-Sadawi, one of them in Morocco and the other in the United States during an academic gathering held in Washington, DC in 1994 at the invitation of the Middle Eastern Studies Association where she came to Islam's defense before hundreds of professors with specializations relating to Middle East studies. Somewhat summarized she said, "You Western professors encourage us to violate our religion and rebel against our culture and civilization, claiming that Islam is hostile to women and their rights. I have witnessed many things among you that bespeak discrimination, prejudice, and condescending attitudes toward other peoples. However, we have nothing comparable to any of this in our religion, our culture, or our traditions."

Apostates most certainly do exist, and there are, undoubtedly, Muslims who have chosen to disassociate themselves from Islam; in this way Islam is purified of its dross. However, one may ask: If this penalty had been carried out completely and consistently throughout the various periods of our history, would the phenomenon of apostasy have ceased to occur? Would Muslim societies today be free of those who have adopted godless intellectual trends and the like, disregarding their Islamic identities and doctrines? Put another way: If the death penalty for apostasy were applied throughout the Muslim world, would those who have spent significant periods of their lives as Marxist-Leninists, secularists, nihilists, or existentialists, then returned to Islam of their own accord, thereby rediscovering their identities and adopting anew the Islamic way of life, be alive today and doing what they are doing to defend Islam: refining and purifying its heritage and traditions, promoting its principles and making its light visible for all to see?

THE CONCEPT OF *ḤADD* IN THE QUR'AN AND ISLAMIC JURISPRUDENCE

In keeping with the custom of Muslim jurists, this study uses the term *ḥadd*[7] throughout this discussion even though the simple term *ʿuqūbah* ('punishment', 'penalty') would have been more fitting, since what is meant by the term *ḥudūd* (the plural of *ḥadd*) in the Qur'an is not 'punishments', but, rather, 'God's laws and rulings.' The Arabs have tended to use the linguistic term *ḥadd* in the sense of a barrier between two things, something which prevents two entities from mingling with each other; however, this is based on their own agreed-upon use of the language. As for the Qur'an, it has its own language, or 'tongue', as it were. An earlier study by this author entitled *Lisān al-Qur'ān wa ʿArabiyyatuhu*,[8] has sought to make clear what is meant by 'the Qur'anic tongue' and its distinguishing features, as well as the points of resemblance and contrast, or agreement and disagreement, between this 'Qur'anic tongue' and 'the Arabic tongue' overall. The terms employed by Muslim jurists and scholars of the fundamentals of jurisprudence have tended to be dominated not by 'the Qur'anic tongue' but, rather, by 'the Arabic tongue.' A salient example of this may be seen in the use of the term *ḥadd* and its plural, *ḥudūd*. This term occurs in fourteen verses of the Qur'an. In two of these, it is used in the sense of 'God's law and commands'; the first reads:

> These are the bounds set by God (*ḥudūd Allāh*); do not, then, offend against them – [for] it is thus that God makes clear His messages unto mankind, so that they might remain conscious of Him. (2:187)

It is clear from the preceding verses (183–186) that what is meant here by "the bounds set by God" is His laws as they relate to fasting and breaking of fasts, and what is permitted and not permitted during a fast.

In the same surah and elsewhere, the term *ḥadd/ḥudūd* is used nine times in connection with God's laws pertaining to marriage and divorce:[9]

> A divorce may be [revoked] twice, whereupon the marriage must either be resumed in fairness or dissolved in a goodly manner. And it is not lawful for you to take back anything of what you have ever given to your wives unless both [partners] have cause to fear that they may not be able to keep within *the bounds set by God* (*ḥudūd Allāh*). Hence, if you have cause to fear that the two may not be able to keep within *the bounds set by God*, there shall be no sin upon either of them for what the wife may give up [to her husband] in order to free herself. These are *the bounds set by God*; do not, then, transgress them; for they who transgress *the bounds set by God* – it is they, they who are evildoers! And if he divorces her [finally], she shall thereafter not be lawful unto him unless the first takes another man for husband. Then, if the latter divorces her, there shall be no sin upon either of the two if they return to one another – provided that both of them think that they will be able to keep within *the bounds set by God*; for these are *the bounds of God* which He makes clear to those of innate knowledge. (2:229–230, *italics added*).

The term appears two times in the first verse of *Sūrah al-Ṭalāq*, where we read:

> O Prophet! When you [intend to] divorce women, divorce them with a view to the waiting-period appointed for them, and reckon the period [carefully], and be conscious of God, your Sustainer. Do not expel them from their homes; and neither shall they [be made to] leave unless they become openly guilty of immoral conduct. These, then, are *the bounds set by God* – and he who transgresses *the bounds set by God* does indeed sin against himself. [For, O man, although] thou knowest it not, after that [first breach] God may well cause something new to come about. (65:1, *italics added*).

It appears twice in connection with God's laws as they pertain to inheritance. God declares:

> These are *the bounds set by God*. And whoever pays heed unto God and His Apostle, him will He bring into gardens through which

running waters flow, therein to abide; and this is a triumph supreme. And whoever rebels against God and His Apostle and transgresses *His bounds*, him will He commit unto fire, therein to abide; and shameful suffering awaits him. (4:13–14, *italics added*).

In *Sūrah al-Mujādalah*, the term occurs once in the verse which deals with the atonement required of a husband who has been guilty of the practice of *ẓihār*:[10]

However, he who does not have the wherewithal [to free a slave from bondage][11] shall fast [instead] for two consecutive months before the couple may touch one another again; and he who is unable to do it shall feed sixty needy ones; this, so that you might prove your faith in God and His Apostle. Now these are *the bounds set by God,* and grievous suffering [in the life to come] awaits all who deny the truth. (58:4, *italics added*).

Lastly, the term occurs in the same sense in two separate verses from *Sūrah al-Tawbah*:

[The hypocrites among] the Bedouins are more tenacious in [their] refusal to acknowledge the truth and in [their] hypocrisy [than are settled people], and more liable to ignore *the ordinances which God has bestowed from on high* (*ḥudūd mā anzala Allāh*) upon His Apostle – but God is All-Knowing, Wise. (9:97, *italics added*).

...and forbid the doing of what is wrong, and keep to *the bounds set by God*. And give thou [O Prophet] the glad tiding [of God's promise] to all believers. (9:112, *italics added*).

These are all of the verses in which the word *ḥudūd* occurs. However, in none of them is it used to refer to a punishment, be it one which is specifically defined within authoritative Islamic texts or one which is left to the discretion of a judge. Rather, in all of the instances cited, the word is used in affirmation of the necessity of adhering to God's ordinances and laws. More specifically, it is used by way of commentary on divine ordinances in relation to which people may be prone to grow lax, since they affect areas of life that are colored by human passions and desires and which could be subject to disagreement and potential conflict. Hence, the only thing that can preserve people and protect them from falling into various types of excess, violations of their own or others' rights, or the abyss of conflict and strife, is obedience to the relevant laws and rulings that God has set forth.

MUSLIM JURISTS AND THEIR USE OF THE TERM *ḤUDŪD*

The above discussion establishes what is meant by the term *ḥadd* or *ḥudūd* in the language of the Qur'an, namely, God's laws and ordinances in a general sense. Moreover, a total of eleven out of the fourteen verses in which the term is used, stress the importance of adhering to God's laws having to do with family-related issues. Hence, one wonders how Muslim jurists shifted the use of this Qur'anic term in such a way that its meaning came to be restricted to the realm of the penal system. The term *ḥadd*, linguistically, means prevention or prohibition. Hence, both a doorman and a prison guard may be referred to as a *ḥaddād*, the former because he prevents people from coming in, and the latter because he prevents people from coming out. Similarly, it has been said that that which defines the essence of something is referred to as a *ḥadd* due to the fact that it prevents the 'entry' [of foreign meanings] and the 'exit' [of relevant significations or features]. God's *ḥudūd* are His prohibitions; as He declares in the passage quoted above in connection with matters relating to fasting, "These are the bounds set by God (*ḥudūd Allāh*): do not, then, offend against them" (2:187).[12] They have said:

> The term *ḥadd*, based on agreed-upon usage, refers to a specified penalty which must be exacted based on a right due to God. Similarly, the term is defined by the Shāfiʿī and Ḥanbalī schools as a specified penalty for a sin which must be exacted from the offender based on a right due to God, as, for example, the punishment for

> sexual misconduct, or offenses which violate both a divine right and a human right, such as a false accusation of sexual misconduct. Such penalties do not include discretionary punishments, which are not laid down specifically in authoritative Islamic texts. Nor do they include penalties meted out based on the law of retaliation (*al-qiṣās*), which has to do with the violation of a solely human right. However, some Muslim jurists define the term *ḥadd* as any penalty which is specified by the Lawgiver Himself, and which therefore includes the law of retaliation.[13]

Based on the foregoing, it may be seen that everything stated in the Qur'an has been excluded from the definition of this Qur'anic concept! A process of blatant despoliation has taken place, as the entire concept has been reduced in such jurists' thinking to nothing more than specified punishments. And this seems utterly amazing.

Virtually none of the penalties mentioned in the Qur'an for theft, sexual misconduct and falsely accusing someone of unchastity is referred to with the term *ḥadd*, and this despite the fact that these punishments are clearly specified. So, why this departure from the language of the Qur'an? After all, do they not say, "An agreed-upon term is incontestable"? And if so, why should this principle not apply to the Qur'an, concerning which no dissension or disagreement is permitted? What lies behind this blatant contravention of Qur'anic usage?

The motive force behind such a violation may lie in the fact that a ruler looks upon the penal system as the most important means of imposing order, commanding respect, and achieving his aims, since it is through the penal system and its associated deterrents that he ensures state security. The most formidable penal system is one whose authority can be attributed to God, since it is through this type of system that the ruler can reap the greatest number of benefits for his regime. At the same time, he will attribute as many of the system's negative aspects as he can to God, despite the fact that any negative aspects which people observe are due not to God's law itself, but, rather, to God's law's having been distorted or incorrectly applied.

Consequently, pious scholars such as Imam Mālik, Abū Ḥanīfah, al-Shāfiʿī, Aḥmad ibn Ḥanbal, al-Ḥasan al-Baṣrī, Sufyān al-Thawrī, and others frequently denounced the ways in which rulers would take the penal system off track, exploiting it for their own tyrannical and capricious ends. One finds such denunciations clearly enunciated in their sermons and exhortations to rulers, as well as in their epistles, lessons, and juristic writings. The written corpus of Muslim heritage thus includes missives penned to rulers by the proponents of justice and the affirmation of God's oneness in which rulers were taken to task for their misuse and arbitrary application of the penal system. Indeed, it has been seen in our own age how some proponents of what has come to be known as 'political Islam' reduce Islam and Islamic law in their entirety to this system alone. Consequently, one finds that when many such individuals speak of applying Islamic law, what they mean by 'Islamic law' is nothing but its associated penalties. Likewise, some regimes are quick to apply certain penalties in order to demonstrate their religious rigor and their commitment to the Shariʿah even when, in reality, the only share they may have in the Shariʿah is these penalties and nothing more.

The foregoing discussion aims to have made clear some of the differences between the purity of the religion itself and the distortions which come about as a result of human religiosity and ways of understanding the religion. Such distortions involve a despoliation of the religion's concepts, which are emptied of their legitimate content and given other meanings.

God declares that the reason He has sent His messengers is in order that people might not have any argument against Him. He states, "[We sent all these] apostles as heralds of glad tidings and as warners, so that men might have no excuse before God after [the coming of] these apostles; and God is indeed, Almighty, Wise" (4:165). In so saying, the majestic Creator is affirming that He has given human beings the capacity to protest and argue and the instinctive desire to seek evidence and proof. Not only this, but God has granted human beings permission to seek these things first and foremost from Him, as well as from His apostles and prophets. How much more, then, is one entitled to seek evidence and proof from others? Even so, half-educated, would-be seekers of knowledge and the general populace merely accept and follow what is proposed to them without question or critical reflection, their minds inoperative and their souls in a state of passivity. Hence, despots and proponents of falsehood play them for fools and wrest obedience from them, while they in turn support such rulers in their deceit and besiege those who would strive for reform and call others to the truth.

The seal of the prophets, Prophet Muhammad, has come, of this there is no doubt for anyone who believes in prophecy, with the exception of the Qadyaniyyah* and others who do not acknowledge the seal of the prophets and continue to await a final prophet, represented among Christians by the final coming of Christ and, among the Jews, by the Messiah. Meanwhile, the Qur'an has remained absolute and unchanging despite the vicissitudes of time and place. The Qur'an thus gives Islam horizons that renew themselves with the passing of the ages; it provides firm grounding for Islam's ageless doctrine and clarifies the principles of its law. Islam is the divinely-inspired religion which God has commanded humankind to profess from the time when revelation was bestowed on the first prophet until the arrival of the seal of the prophets, who brought it anew with a more inclusive, universal meaning, and with a constantly evolving understanding of the Qur'an, the Book of God, the Infinite and Eternal. Taken as a whole, the life and example of the Messenger of God exemplify a way of following the truth as it ought to be followed and a model for understanding and emulation based thereon rather than a kind of blind, superficial imitation. Islam, with its final rules and principles as enshrined in the Qur'an, is the religion of God, as a result of which there is no other religion that God will accept from His creatures. This, moreover, requires that the Qur'an be given supremacy over all else. After all, no human understanding, from whatever age or generation it arises, can encompass all the meanings of the Qur'an or place them in set, final molds that allow for no other understanding. Otherwise, the Qur'an would lose its absolute, all-inclusive nature and be transformed, instead, into a relative, historically bound text with relevance only to its own time and place, whose meanings can be manipulated through explanations and human interpretations subject to the vicissitudes of time, place, human caprice, events, customs, cultures and traditions.

For this reason, the Messenger of God did not restrict or qualify the meanings of the Qur'an with a final interpretation or exegesis of his own.[14] Rather, through his obedience to the Qur'an, his teaching, his life and his example, he embodied the contents of the Book and its ordinances in a way that set forth what might be termed 'the methodology of emulation and obedience' which God has commanded people to adhere to. This applies to the verses which contain legal rulings, and which come, at the most, to one out of every twelve verses in the Qur'an. As for what remains of the Qur'an, it consists for the most part of unqualified verses which encompass all times and places, with the result that those living in any and every age can benefit from their meanings to the extent that God opens up to them their hidden content through openhearted contemplation. Thus, in those aspects that do not touch upon legal rulings and the necessary, direct explication of verses from the Qur'an, particularly in its practical aspect, the Sunnah constitutes an application of the Qur'an that reflects the highest, most accurate degree of understanding thereof. In its confirmatory* and verbal aspects, the Sunnah represents the most precise possible elucidation of the verses of the Qur'an next to the Qur'an's elucidation of itself. In sum, then, the Sunnah, taken as a whole, offers the methodology of emulation of the Prophet. Hence, we need to realize the major differences between emulation and obedience on the one hand, and imitation and uncritical acceptance on the other. Emulation and obedience are processes that rest upon the authoritative nature and persuasiveness of the evidence and one's knowledge and understanding thereof. As for imitation and uncritical acceptance (*al-taqlīd*), they are a kind of unthinking mimicry unpreceded by any examination of or reflection on relevant evidence.

Seen against the backdrop of the absoluteness and conclusiveness of the Qur'an, our entire heritage may be said to fall within the domain of the relative, which is subject to the influence of temporal and geographical factors and the specific cultural and intellectual environment of the person engaging in the process of interpretation. When one realizes this fact and come to appreciate the unique features of Islam's eternal, final message and the religion's governing values, legal intents and spiritual aims, one will be able to discover a great many areas of weakness in our heritage along with a great many areas of strength.

EXEGESIS, THE SCIENCES OF INTENTS, AND EXTERNAL INFLUENCES

One of the distinctive features of Islamic law is that it involves a coupling of *ᶜaql*, that is, evidence based on reason, with *samᶜ*, or evidence based on authoritative texts; similarly, it consists of *sharᶜ*, that is, explicit ordinances and *ra'y*, or human interpretations of such ordinances. It is by drawing on all of these, both individually and taken together, that we are guided along the right path. Ijtihad, or independent reasoning, reform, and resistance to innovations which represent a departure from Islam's intents and teachings, are not exceptional measures to which one resorts only when absolutely necessary. Rather, they are basic, essential measures concerning which the Muslim community was addressed at the time when it first received the Islamic revelation. This is a vital fact to which attention needs to be drawn if we are to overcome a certain long-held erroneous notion, namely, that ijtihad is a process to which a scholar resorts only when he finds no explicit text in either the Qur'an or the Sunnah that rules on the question or incident with which he is concerned. For although a jurist will, in fact, resort to ijtihad in such a situation, it should be remembered that reflection on the Sunnah as that which clarifies, explicates and applies the Qur'an likewise requires ijtihad, and to the very same degree.

The sharing and mingling of culture and knowledge, by whatever terms we choose to refer to this phenomenon, is a process that takes place naturally among nations and peoples. After all, the earth is a vast, extended home for the human family just as the human family itself is a single, extended entity. As for differences of climate, terrain, language, skin color and so forth, these have been brought into being in order for each group of people to recognize its own realm and in order to build up, within this realm, the type of civilization best suited to its disposition and needs, since these are the things that set one group of people apart from every other. It comes as no surprise, then, that interaction and intermingling have taken place during the various phases of history on the levels of thought, knowledge, culture and civilization. The establishment of boundaries is an illusory process that people undertake in an attempt to set their own territories apart from those of others, to enjoy a sense of uniqueness, to satisfy their need for a sense of ownership, and to see the fruits of their efforts within a delimited sphere. And in so doing, one society or group of people moves others to do as they have done and to strive to achieve the same degree of development and prosperity in their own territories.

2

THE QUR'ANIC DESCRIPTION OF APOSTASY

THE CONCEPT OF APOSTASY IN THE QUR'AN

The following passages shed light on the fundamental features of the concept of apostasy as presented in the Qur'an:

[ONE]: "If any of you should turn away from his faith and die as a denier of the truth – these it is whose works will go for nought in this world and in the life to come; and these it is who are destined for the fire, therein to abide" (2:217). For those who commit apostasy, their works both in this life and in the life to come are rendered worthless.

[TWO]: "How would God bestow His guidance upon people who have resolved to deny the truth after having attained to faith, and having borne witness that this Apostle is true, and [after] all evidence of the truth has come unto them? For, God does not guide such evil-doing folk" (3:86). Apostasy entails the negation of right guidance and the willingness to receive it.

[THREE]: "Verily, as for those who are bent on denying the truth after having attained to faith, and then grow [ever more stubborn] in their refusal to acknowledge the truth, their repentance shall not be accepted" (3:90). Repeated apostasy prevents one's repentance from being accepted.

[FOUR]: "Verily, as for those who are bent on denying the truth and die as deniers of the truth – not all the gold on earth could ever be their ransom. It is they for whom grievous suffering is in store; and they shall have none to succor them" (3:91). The divine punishment for dying in a state of unbelief will not be rescinded by virtue of any [good] work one has performed in this earthly life, nor by any ransom one might offer in return for one's redemption. The statement made in this verse also contains a hypothetical element given that, once he has died, the apostate will have nowhere from which to obtain "all the gold on earth."

[FIVE]: "O you who have attained to faith! If you pay heed to some of those to whom revelation was vouchsafed aforetime, they might cause you to renounce the truth after you have come to believe [in it]" (3:98). There are those who would induce the weak to commit apostasy.

[SIX]: "...on the Day [of Judgment] when some faces will shine [with happiness] and some faces will be dark [with grief]. And as for those with faces darkened, [they shall be told]: 'Did you deny the truth after having attained to faith? Taste, then, this suffering for having denied the truth!'" (3:106). This verse describes some of the grievous chastisement that awaits those who turn away from their faith.

[SEVEN]: "Verily, they who have bought a denial of the truth at the price of faith can in no wise harm God, whereas grievous suffering awaits them" (3:177). The person who commits apostasy hurts only himself.

[EIGHT]: "O you who have attained to faith! If you ever abandon your faith, God will in time bring forth [in your stead] people whom He loves and who love Him" (5:54). The person who turns away from faith does not love God, but will not be able to bring Him harm in any way; rather, God will replace him with those who are better than he is.

[NINE]: "Behold, as for those who come to believe, and then deny the truth, and again come to believe, and again deny the truth, and thereafter grow stubborn in their denial of the truth – God will not forgive them, nor will He guide them in any way" (4:137). Those who turn away from their faith repeatedly will not be able to attain to God's forgiveness no matter what they do.

[TEN]: "As for anyone who denies God after having once attained to faith – and this, to be sure, does not apply to one who does it under duress, the while his heart remains true to his faith, but [only to] him who willingly opens up his heart to a denial of the truth – : upon all such [falls] God's condemnation, and tremendous suffering awaits them" (16:106). Apostasy committed by someone who has done so under duress, and who therefore had no other choice, does not affect his actual faith. The only way in which apostasy can affect one's actual faith is for one to open his or her heart consciously and willingly to a denial of the truth.

[ELEVEN]: "And there is, too, among men many a one who worships God on the border-line [of faith]; thus, if good befalls him, he is satisfied with Him; but if a trial assails him, he turns away utterly, losing [thereby both] this world and the life to come: [and] this, indeed, is a loss beyond compare!" (22:11). Weak faith, lack of certainty and failure to worship God with a pure heart are among the most important entry points for apostasy.

[TWELVE]: "Verily, they who are bent on denying the truth and on barring [others] from the path of God, and [who thus] cut themselves off from the Apostle after guidance has been vouchsafed to them, can in no wise harm God; but He will cause all their deeds to come to nought" (47:32). Unbelief cannot harm God in any way; rather, whatever works are performed by the person who denies the truth will come to nothing, and this is the outcome he or she must expect.

All these verses taken together serve to expound the essence of apostasy (*al-riddah* or *al-irtidād*). The term 'apostasy' conveys the sense of turning away from Islam and faith after one's having accepted them in accordance with what God has commanded. This act of turning away includes a retreat from Islam and faith to a religion which the apostate had professed at some previous time, a shift to some other, third, religion, as well as the adoption of atheism and a lack of faith in any religion. All such states are a retreat from Islam, and they are all examples of apostasy. It thus becomes clear that the terms *al-riddah* and *al-irtidād* in the Qur'anic understanding represent a return to something one had left from something one had reached. However, in none of the varied contexts in which the Qur'an refers to apostasy does it speak of it as a withdrawal from Islam alone, or as a withdrawal relating to the spiritual plane alone. Rather, it uses the term in a manner which is inclusive of both the spiritual and the material.

In his book entitled, *Al-Mufradāt fī Gharīb al-Qur'ān*, al-Rāghib al-Iṣfahānī makes reference to these two aspects of the Qur'anic usage, saying:

> The verb *radda* means "to avert or turn away something in and of itself, or in one of its states." One might say, "I averted it," or "I brought it back" (*radadtuhu*), as a result of which "it was averted," or, "it was brought back" (*irtadda*). God declares, "His punishment shall not be averted (*lā yuraddu*) from people who are lost in sin" (6:147). In a reference to the bringing back of something in itself, God declares, "...and if they were brought back (*ruddū*) [to life], they would return to the very thing which was forbidden to them" (6:28); "And after a time We allowed you to prevail against them once again (*radadnā lakum al-karrah*) (17:6)"; "Bring them back (*ruddūhā*) unto me!" (38:33); "And thus We restored him (*radadnāhu*) to his mother" (28:13); "...'Oh, would that we were brought back (*nuraddu*) [to life]; then we would not give the lie to our Sustainer's messages...'" (6:27).
>
> Examples of the use of the word *radda* in the sense of reverting to a previous state include: "...they will cause you to turn back (*yaruddūkum*) on your heels..." (3:149); "...and if He intends good for thee, there is none who could turn away (*lā rādda*) His bounty" (10:107) meaning that there is no one who could prevent His bounty from being given; we also have the words, "verily, there shall fall

upon them a chastisement which none can avert (*ʿadhāb ghayr mardūd*)" (11:76).

The word may also be used in the sense of a return to God: "But even if I am brought (*wa la'in rudidtu*) before my Sustainer, I will surely find something even better than this as [my last] resort" (18:36); "...and then you will be brought back (*turaddūn*) unto Him who knows all that is beyond the reach of a created being's perception as well as all that can be witnessed by a creature's senses or mind" (62:8); "...brought before God (*ruddū ilā Allāh*), their true Lord Supreme" (6:62). Hence, the verb *radda* is like the verb 'return' (*rajaʿa*): "...whereupon unto Him you will be brought back (*thumma ilayhi turjaʿūn*)" (2:28).

There are those who have put forward two different senses of the verb *radda*. The first of these is that of being brought back to what is referred to in the following verse: "Out of this [earth] have We created you, and into it shall We return you (*wa fīhā nuʿīdukum*)" (20:55). As for the second, it is that of being brought back to life as in the words: "...and out of it shall We bring you forth once again" (20:55). In other words, there are two different states, both of which are included in the term's overall sense. We read, "...they covered their mouths with their hands (*raddū aydīhim ilā afwāhihim*)" (14:9). This phrase has been interpreted to mean that they bit their fingertips in rage, or that they gestured to others to be quiet by pointing to their mouths. It has also been said to mean that they placed their hands over the mouths of the prophets in order to silence them. Be that as it may, the use of the verb *radda* indicates that they repeated the action several times.

We read in the Qur'an that "...many among the followers of earlier revelation would like to bring you back (*fa yaruddūnakum*) to denying the truth after you have attained to faith" (2:109). In other words, they would like to bring you back into a state of unbelief after your having left it. The same sense of the word may be seen in the phrase: "O you who have attained to faith! If you pay heed to some of those to whom revelation was vouchsafed aforetime, they might cause you to renounce the truth after you have come to believe [in it] (*yaruddūkum baʿda īmānikum kāfirīn*)" (3:100).

As for *al-irtidād*, it is the same as *al-riddah*, that is, going back the way one came. However, whereas the word *riddah* is used only in connection with apostasy, the word *irtidād* is used in connection with other things as well. The Qur'an speaks of "those who turn their backs (*irtaddū ʿalā adbārihim*) after guidance has been vouchsafed to them..." (47:25); and says, "O you who have attained to faith! If you ever abandon your faith (*man yartadda minkum ʿan dīnihi*)..." (5:54], where it is used to refer to a retreat from Islam into a denial of the truth. The word appears in other verses also, for example: "If any of you should turn away from his faith (*man yartadid minkum ʿan dīnihi*) and die as a denier of the truth..." (2:217); "...and the two turned back (*irtaddā*), retracing their footsteps..." (18:64); "those who turn their backs (*irtaddū ʿalā adbārihim*) after guidance has been vouchsafed to them..." (47:25); "...and turn around on our heels (*wa nuraddu ʿala aʿqābinā*) after God has guided us aright!" (6:71); "...but do not turn back (*lā tartaddū ʿalā adbārikum*), for then you will be lost" (5:21), which is to say: If you investigate something and find it to be good, do not turn away from it. Similarly we read: "But when the bearer of good tidings came [with Joseph's tunic], he laid it over his face; and he regained his sight (*irtadda baṣīran*)" (12:96).

Someone might say, "I have referred judgment (*radadtu al-ḥukm*) on such-and-such to so-and-so," which means, "I have authorized him to make this judgment." God says, "...if they would but refer it unto the Apostle (*law raddūhu ilā al-rasūl*) and unto those from among the believers who have been entrusted with authority..." (4:83); "...and if you are at variance over any matter, refer it unto God and the Apostle (*ruddūhu ilā Allāh wa al-rasūl*)" (4:59).

One might say, *rāddahu fī kalāmihi*, meaning, "He took issue with what he said," or "He discussed with him what he had said." There is a hadith in which we read, *al-bayᶜāni yatarāddān*, meaning that after a sale has been concluded, each of the two parties to the transaction takes back what he had given to the other. The phrase *raddat al-ibl* refers to a camel's coming back to the water repeatedly to drink; as for the phrase *araddat al-nāqah*, it refers to a she-camel's coming back to drink to the point where the creases in her body fill out and her private parts are swollen. And lastly, if one says *istaradda al-matāᶜ*, it means that someone recovered something that belongs to him.[1]

APOSTASY AS A RETREAT TO SOMETHING ONE HAS LEFT, OR TO SOMETHING ELSE

As shown above, the term *riddah* in the Qur'an means an explicit retreat from and abandonment of Islam after one's having entered it. All commentators on the Qur'an have interpreted it to mean a retreat from Islam to unbelief, pointing out that the verses dealing with it communicate a warning to those who have entered Islam against abandoning it or taking lightly the thought of doing so. At the same time, these verses urge everyone who has entered Islam to cling to it steadfastly because it is the true guidance which is the most authoritative, solid basis for life and living; it means integrity along the path, and proceeding through life on the basis of the manifest truth which keeps those who follow it from losing their way. This is the view put forward by al-Qurṭubī in his exegesis of Qur'an 2:217; he is followed in this view by al-Zamakhsharī, who affirms that this and similar verses address a warning to Muslims, urging them to persevere in Islam and to die as Muslims. This view is likewise expressed by al-Ṭabarsī, al-Ālūsī, al-Nīsābūrī, al-Bayḍāwī and al-Ṭabarī in *Jāmiᶜ al-Bayān*.

Given this clarification of the concept of apostasy, or *riddah,* in the Qur'an, we can see how the Qur'an has put this linguistic term to use to convey a variety of meanings by employing it as a verbal noun related to the religion. *Lisān al-ᶜArab* lists the word *irtadda* and the phrase *irtadda ᶜan* as meaning "to shift, switch, change." It is likewise used in the Qur'anic revelation in the phrase, "If you ever abandon your faith (*man yartadid minkum ʿan dīnihi*)" (5:54). The verbal noun *al-riddah* is used to refer to a retreat from Islam. A person abandons his faith if he denies the truth after having surrendered himself to God through Islam.[2] This explanation finds agreement in *al-Qāmūs* [by Fayrūz Ābādī], in *Tāj al-ʿArūs* [by al-Zubaydī, who expounds on *al-Qāmūs*] and, before them, in *al-Ṣiḥāḥ* by al-Jawharī, and in *al-Jawharah* by al-Azdī, as well as all other Arabic dictionaries both ancient and modern. *Al-Nihāyah* by Ibn al-Athīr, *al-Miṣbāḥ al-Munīr* and *Asās al-Balāghah* all agree that the person who engages in the act of *irtidād* is someone who turns back, retraces his steps, or leaves the path he has been traveling. The word can be used to describe anyone who retreats from something in which he was engaged or to which he was committed, be it a religion or some other good. This sense of the word may be found in the Qur'an, where we read that, "...the two turned back (*irtaddā*), retracing their footsteps..." (18:64). In other words, they went back down the path they had trodden. Hence, the apostate (*al-murtadd*) is referred to as such because of his having turned back on the religion which he had professed. The use of this term indicates that when a person believes and turns his face to God, it is as though he were traveling a path to reach Him. Hence, when apostasy occurs, it is as though the person were going back down the path he had been following to reach God. Thus it is fitting that the action should be referred to as *riddah*, and that the person who engages in this action should be referred to as *murtadd*.

The word *riddah*, then, is a religious legal term which is applied correctly to this type of retreat. Consequently, there is no longer any need for us to state whether this term refers to a retreat from Islam, or a whether it constitutes a general linguistic term with the unqualified sense of 'retreat,' since it has been used over the centuries in such a way that it has come to refer unambiguously to a retreat from religion, and specifically, from the religion of Islam.

None of the aforementioned verses – which include everything the Qur'an has to say concerning either *riddah* or *irtidād* – makes any mention of an earthly punishment for the sin or crime of apostasy; nor do they refer, whether explicitly or implicitly, to the need to force an apostate to return to Islam or to kill him if he refuses to do so. The Qur'an mentions this crime in numerous different contexts, in some of which it treats *irtidād* in its linguistic significations, making clear that it is an unqualified retreat to a point which had been passed at some previous time as though the apostate (*al-murtadd*) were turning on his heels, thereby forfeiting all the fruits of the efforts he had once exerted when he passed the starting point. He had been laboring and striving to meet his Lord, only to withdraw once again to where he started.

In other contexts, the Qur'an uses the term *riddah* or *irtidād* in a specifically religious, technical sense, thereby charging it with those meanings which pertain to Islamic law, yet without causing its linguistic form to lose its flexibility and its ability to accommodate the sense of retreating to an unspecified starting point. In the case of someone who apostatizes from Islam, however, he or she nullifies all the efforts he or she made to get past the point at which he or she surrendered to God, thereby negating the value of the years he/she spent moving in the direction of full surrender to God. As portrayed in the Qur'an, the term *riddah* reflects the psychological and mental state which brought the individual concerned to the point of apostasy. The least that can be said about this state is that it is one of anxiety, unrest, lostness and error which have taken the individual over so fully that he has beaten a retreat, no longer capable of carrying on with his journey and his progress toward God and Paradise. Such a person no longer knows how to move forward in order to realize the goal after having once known the way and even covered part of the distance. He is a miserable, wretched human being who deserves to be pitied, and is not worthy to be faithful to the divine covenant. In other words, he is unable to bear the 'trust', to carry out the tasks entailed by being God's vicegerent on earth, or to endure the testing that comes with the life of faith. As a consequence, he is in a state of such constant angst and vacillation that he would not be capable of bearing up under tribulation, living out Islam's higher values, or fulfilling its intents. It is as though the Qur'an views the apostate as being of too little significance to be punished in this life, or for God Almighty to issue legislation defining a worldly punishment for him.

Rather, his distress, confusion, anxiety, vacillation, and constant fear of the unknown render him unworthy of being subjected to an earthly penalty. After all, the legally prescribed punishments in Islam are designed not only to discipline the offender, but, in addition, to serve as purifying atonements. However, the apostate is someone who is not worthy of any of this in the present life; rather, the fire is more fitting for him, and he for the fire. In this life, the torment of apprehension, irresolution, insecurity, psychological instability and the loss of mental integrity, tranquility and inner peace are sufficient punishment for him.

RELIGIOUS FREEDOM AS A CHIEF INTENT OF ISLAMIC LAW

Human freedom is one of the supreme values of Islamic law, and one of its most vital intents. Indeed, one of the most noteworthy roles played by faith, and by the affirmation of God's oneness in particular, is to free human beings from superstition, paganism, and the worship of created entities and to link them with God Almighty in such a way that they fear no one but God, seek His help alone, and turn their faces fully to Him. In affirmation of this message, and in order to liberate people fully, many Qur'anic verses were revealed in support, defense and protection of this freedom, which is the essence of our humanity. Indeed, so essential is this freedom that if we were to lose it, we would forfeit our role in the universe and in existence.

These verses, which number more than two hundred, begin by illustrating the meaning of true, worshipful submission to God, and by comparing this with the worship of entities other than Him. In this way, God makes clear to us that worshipping and serving Him are the source of true liberation and dignity, not of humiliation and degradation. He says:

> ...and will [people continue to] worship, instead of God, something that has it not within its power to provide for them any sustenance whatever from the heavens or the earth, and can do nothing at all? Hence, do not coin any similitudes for God! Verily, God knows [all],

whereas you have no [real] knowledge. God propounds [to you] the parable of [two men -]: a man enslaved, unable to do anything of his own accord, and a [free] man upon whom We have bestowed goodly sustenance [as a gift] from Ourselves, so that he can spend thereof [at will, both] secretly and openly. Can these [two] be deemed equal? All praise is due to God [alone]: but most of them do not understand it.

And God propounds [to you] the parable of two [other] men – one of them dumb, unable to do anything of his own accord, and a sheer burden on his master: to whichever task the latter directs him, he accomplishes no good. Can such a one be considered the equal of [a wise man] who enjoins the doing of what is right and himself follows a straight way?

And God's [alone] is the knowledge of the hidden reality of the heavens and the earth. And so, the advent of the Last Hour will but manifest itself [in a single moment,] like the twinkling of an eye, or, closer still: for, behold, God has the power to will anything.

And God has brought you forth from your mothers' wombs, knowing nothing – but He has endowed you with hearing, and sight, and minds, so that you might have cause to be grateful. (16:73–78)

The types of freedom upon which the Qur'an places the highest value, which it guarantees to human beings and which it enjoins us to preserve, are the freedom of belief and the freedom of expression. These are then followed by all other freedoms which preserve our humanity.

Numerous Qur'anic verses stress the necessity of preserving human freedoms in relation to supreme values such as belief in God's oneness, purification, development, prosperity and civilization and the intents of Islamic law related thereto, such as justice, freedom, equality and the like. The Qur'an thus stresses human freedom, particularly the freedom to choose what we will believe, and the impermissibility of compelling anyone to adopt a particular belief or to replace one belief with another. It affirms that doctrine is a private matter between the individual and his Lord, as a result of which no one has the right under any circumstances, or in any way – including the exploitation of a human being's need, the presentation of material enticements or anything of the sort – to compel another person to accept a particular belief or to change his beliefs.[3]

THE OCCASION AND MEANINGS OF THE VERSE: "THERE SHALL BE NO COERCION IN MATTERS OF FAITH"

The many Qur'anic verses devoted to religious freedom support one another in asserting this right and the obligation to protect and preserve it from any external intervention or interference. Foremost among these verses is the one which declares:

> There shall be no coercion in matters of faith. Distinct has now become the right way from the way of error; hence, he who rejects the powers of evil and believes in God has indeed taken hold of a support most unfailing, which shall never give way: for God is All-Hearing, All-Knowing. (2:256)

In his *Tafsīr al-Manār*, Rashid Rida mentions the reason for which this verse was revealed. In so doing, he leaves no room for claims to the effect that this verse has been abrogated, or for interpretations that are not in keeping with its inclusive nature. In explaining the reason for its having been revealed, Rida states:

> Women whose infants had died would sometimes make a pledge that, if a child of theirs survived, they would convert him or her to Judaism. When the Jewish tribe of Banū al-Naḍīr were expelled, there were children of the Anṣār[4] among them, and they said, "We will not allow our children [to remain Jews and be thus expelled]," after which God revealed, "There shall be no coercion in matters of faith." Based on an account passed down on the authority of Ibn ʿAbbās and with a chain of transmission that includes ʿIkrimah, Ibn

> Jarīr states that this verse was revealed concerning a man of the tribe of Banū Sālim by the name of al-Ḥusayn who was one of the Anṣār, and who had two Christian sons. Being a Muslim himself, he said to the Prophet, "Shall I not compel them [to embrace Islam]? Neither of them will accept any religion but Christianity," after which God revealed this verse. According to some commentaries, al-Ḥusayn tried to convert his sons by force, whereupon they brought a complaint before the Prophet. He [al-Ḥusayn] then said, "O Messenger of God, shall my own flesh and blood enter the fire while I look on?" However, the Prophet would not give him permission to force his two sons to enter Islam. Ibn Jarīr narrates several accounts concerning women in the pre-Islamic era who pledged to convert their children to Judaism in order for them to survive. He also relates accounts according to which, after the advent of Islam, Muslims wanted to force their children who were either Christians or Jews to embrace Islam, in response to which this verse was revealed, and it served as the decisive word on the matter. An account related by Ibn Jarīr on the authority of Saʿīd ibn Jubayr tells us that when this verse was revealed, the Prophet said, "God has given your Companions a choice: If they choose you, they will belong to you, and if they choose them, they will belong to them."[5]

Rashid Rida states in his commentary, "This is the verdict issued by Islam, many of whose enemies claim that it was established by the sword, and that it was presented to people with force to back it up. According to this claim, if one accepted Islam, one survived, and if one rejected it, the sword carried out its verdict against him." Was the sword at work in coercing people to embrace Islam in Makkah during the days when the Prophet was having to pray in hiding, and during the days when the polytheists were putting the Muslims to the test with all manner of torture to the point where the Prophet and his Companions had no choice but emigrate? Or do they say that the alleged coercion took place in Madinah after Islam came into its glory, and that this verse was revealed at the height of this glory and strength? The Battle of Banū al-Naḍīr took place in the month of Rabīʿ al-Awwal in the year 4 AH.[6] The unbelievers in Makkah were waging war on the Muslims when Banū al-Naḍīr broke their covenant with the Prophet and plotted against him, making two assassination attempts against him while they were living as his neighbors on the outskirts of Madinah. Consequently, it was necessary that they be expelled from the city. The Prophet laid siege to them until he had driven them out, whereupon they left in defeat. Even so, when some of his Companions asked his permission to compel their children who had embraced Judaism to enter Islam, thereby preventing them from leaving with the Jews, the Prophet refused to allow them to do so. This was the first time it had even occurred to the Muslims to try to force anyone to embrace Islam. However, Rida notes, it was customary among the followers of some religions, and Christianity in particular, to force people to convert to their faith.

This issue has more to do with politics than religion. After all, faith, which is the origin and essence of religion, is a kind of inward, voluntary submission, and it goes without saying that voluntary submission couldn't possibly be brought about by force. Rather, it comes about through explanation and proof. This is why the Almighty declares, "Distinct has now become the right way from the way of error" (2:256). That is to say, it has become apparent that this religion contains good sense, right guidance, salvation, and progress along the path of light, and that those religions and sects that conflict with it are in error.[7] The Qur'an affirms that it is the Creator alone who may judge those who call upon entities other than Him. Hence He states, "...he who invokes, side by side with God, any other deity [– a deity] for whose existence he has no evidence – shall but find his reckoning with his Sustainer: [and] verily, such deniers of the truth will never attain to a happy state!" (23:117). At the same time, He addresses the Messenger of God, saying, "And so, exhort them: thy task is only to exhort; thou canst not compel them to believe" (88:21–22); "...thou canst by no means force them [to believe]. Yet nonetheless, remind, through this Qur'an, all such as may fear My warning" (50:45); and, "...thy duty is no more than to deliver the message; and the reckoning is Ours" (13:40).

Many Qur'anic verses make clear to the Prophet that compulsion and the imposition of beliefs on others are of no use whatsoever, and that had God Almighty known that faith could be brought about through compulsion, He would have commanded His messengers to force people to believe and surrender themselves to Him: "Yet if God had so willed, they would not have ascribed divinity to aught beside Him; hence, We have not made thee their keeper, and neither art thou responsible for their conduct" (6:107); "And [thus it is:] had thy Sustainer so willed, all those who live on earth would surely have attained to faith, all of them; dost thou, then, think that thou couldst compel people to believe?" (10:99). God thus makes clear that the matter of doctrine and belief cannot be subjected to any kind of coercion, even if such coercion is motivated by the believer's concern for the one being called to faith and the desire to deliver him from error. God states, "Yet – however strongly thou mayest desire it – most people will not believe [in this revelation]" (12:103). Consequently, God urges the Prophet to issue the call to faith with wisdom, goodly exhortation and arguments presented in a gracious manner, saying, "Call thou [all mankind] unto thy Sustainer's path with wisdom and goodly exhortation, and argue with them in the most kindly manner; for, behold, thy Sustainer knows best as to who strays from His path, and best knows He as to who are the right-guided" (16:125).

From the foregoing it will be clear that religious freedom is hedged about by all the Qur'anic guarantees needed to render it an absolute, unbounded freedom to choose one's beliefs, and that the right to pass judgment on such matters belongs to God alone.

ORIGINAL UNBELIEF VS. UNBELIEF AFTER EMBRACING ISLAM

A distinction might be drawn between the Qur'anic attitude toward continuing in 'original unbelief', that is, the unbelief of someone who has never had faith, and its attitude toward the unbelief of someone who abandons faith for unbelief after having believed. Such a distinction acknowledges the freedom that the Qur'an accords to the person who is still in a state of original unbelief, while denying the same freedom to someone who abandons faith after having believed. God declares, "But whoever chooses to deny the [evidence of the] truth, instead of believing in it, has already strayed from the right path" (2:108); and, "Out of their selfish envy, many among the followers of earlier revelation would like to bring you back to denying the truth after you have attained to faith – [even] after the truth has become clear unto them. Nonetheless, forgive and forbear, until God shall make manifest His will: behold, God has the power to will anything" (2:109); and, "[Your enemies] will not cease to fight against you till they turn you away from your faith, if they can. But if any of you should turn away from his faith and die as a denier of the truth – these it is whose works will go for nought in this world and in the life to come; and these it is who are destined for the fire, therein to abide" (2:217). In a similar vein God declares:

> How would God bestow His guidance upon people who have resolved to deny the truth after having attained to faith, and having borne witness that this Apostle is true, and [after] all evidence of the truth has come unto them? For God does not guide such evildoing folk. Their requital shall be rejection by God, and by the angels, and by all [righteous] men. In this state shall they abide; [and] neither will their suffering be lightened, nor will they be granted respite. But excepted shall be they that afterwards repent and put themselves to right; for, behold, God is Much-Forgiving, a Dispenser of grace. Verily, as for those who are bent on denying the truth after having attained to faith, and then grow [even more stubborn] in their refusal to acknowledge the truth, their repentance shall not be accepted. (3:86–90)

These verses should be taken together with the others of relevance which have already been mentioned. All of these verses, and many others besides, affirm that the person who commits apostasy is threatened with punishment in the afterlife. However, as explicit as all of these verses are, not one of them makes any mention of a legally prescribed, earthly punishment for apostasy, be it execution or anything less drastic. The reason for this is that the authority of the Qur'an is an authority of amelioration and mercy which affirms religious freedom and the need to protect and preserve it. It is an authority which affirms that faith and unbelief are matters of the heart between the servant and his Lord and that the penalty for unbelief and apostasy after one has believed is one that takes effect in the life to come, jurisdiction over which belongs to God alone. As for questions relating to repentance following apostasy and whether or not such repentance will be accepted or not, all these are matters of divine prerogative. As long as one's apostasy has not been accompanied by anything else that would be deemed a criminal act, it remains strictly between God and the individual, and is not the province of earthly rulers or anyone else.

At the same time, the Qur'an makes clear what a serious crime apostasy is and what an injustice the individual does to himself by means of it: by overstepping the bounds of his human finitude and committing the most serious form of wrongdoing, namely, *shirk*, or association of partners with God: "Do not ascribe divine powers to aught beside God; for, behold, such [a false] ascribing of divinity is indeed an awesome wrong" (31:13). The verses of the Qur'an make clear that whoever falls into apostasy sinks into the mire of unbelief. Such verses were revealed to manifest the heinousness of apostasy; however, they do not mention any earthly punishment for it: "And never does thy Sustainer forget [anything]" (19:64).

3

APOSTASY DURING THE PROPHET'S LIFE

PREFATORY REMARKS

Before discussing the details of the Sunnah and the hadiths that have come down to us in connection with the issue of apostasy, let the readers be reminded of something which, in Islam, is an axiomatic truth, namely, that the Qur'an is the foundational source for every one of the doctrines, laws, systems, principles and rules which go to make up the religion of Islam. The Qur'an is a revelation from God, since it is His very words. As for the Sunnah, it is a clarification and explanation of the Qur'an, an exemplar of how to submit to its teachings, and an application of what the Qur'an has enjoined, since the Prophet was sent in order to make clear to people what had been bestowed upon them from on high, to teach them the book and wisdom, and to purify them through their emulation of him.

There are numerous differences between the Qur'an and the Sunnah. The Qur'an, to begin with, is a foundational source for Islamic legal rulings, whereas the authentic Sunnah is a binding source of clarification of what is stated in the Qur'an. The Qur'an and the Sunnah are mutually supporting sources of evidence which are joined by a link of such perfect complementarity that it would be impossible for any part of either of them to contradict or negate the other. There can be no conflict, contradiction, inconsistency or disagreement between them, nor could any part of either them abrogate or nullify what is stated in the other. After all, neither abrogation nor nullification is a clarification; on the contrary, it is an elimination and a cancellation, the very idea of which is unacceptable.[1]

Consequently, it is an impossibility, both logical and legal, for the Sunnah to contain anything which would contradict, much less abrogate, the principles or methods of the Qur'an in any way whatsoever. Whatever is affirmed in the Qur'an is clarified by the Sunnah if people need clarification thereof. This clarification may come through something the Prophet said, something he did in association with something he said, something he did as a means of clarifying how to apply the Qur'an, or his approval of an action or word on someone else's part. In addition, the Sunnah supports and complements what is found in the Qur'an. What is found in the Sunnah can be nothing other than this: an explanation and clarification of the Qur'an in keeping with its principles. How could it be otherwise, when the mission of the Messenger of God was to deliver the message found in the Qur'an, to clarify it in the way that had been set down by the Creator, to recite it and teach it to people, and to purify them by means of it?

The principles and epistemic methodology of the Qur'an clearly specify the unqualified nature of religious freedom. The Qur'an hedges this freedom about with safeguards and guarantees in no fewer than two hundred verses, and states clearly that the punishment to be meted out to the unbeliever or the apostate is one that will take effect in the afterlife. Moreover, as we have stated, one could not expect the Sunnah to conflict with what we find in the Qur'an, especially in view of the fact that this matter is mentioned not in one or two verses, but in approximately two hundred of its definitive verses, all of which unanimously affirm religious freedom.

The Prophet's era witnessed literally hundreds of those who believed, then became hypocrites or committed apostasy. In fact, their apostasy reached the point where it represented a source of harm to the Messenger of God and the Muslim community. Moreover, these people's identities were known to the Messenger of God, who had been given authority, particularly after his emigration to Madinah, to ward off the threat that they posed. However, he refrained from doing them any harm lest it be said that "Muhammad kills his Companions", imposes his doctrine on people, or forces them to embrace his religion. Of relevance in this connection is the account concerning ʿAbd Allāh ibn Ubayy (Ibn Salūl) and his son ʿAbd Allāh. The latter was among the most worthy and virtuous of the Prophet's Companions and had taken part in the battles of Badr and Uḥud as well as all other battles waged by the Messenger of God. Before the advent of Islam, the tribe of Khazraj had agreed unanimously among themselves that they would crown ʿAbd Allāh's father, ʿAbd Allāh ibn Ubayy, as their chief. With the coming of the Prophet, however, they went back on this decision, and ʿAbd Allāh ibn Ubayy became envious of him. In his pride he claimed outwardly to be a Muslim while secretly harboring evil intentions against the Prophet, Islam and Muslims. The words spoken by ʿAbd Allāh ibn Ubayy immediately after the campaign against the tribe of Banū al-Muṣṭaliq are reported by God in the Qur'an, where we read: "[And] they say, 'Indeed, when we return to the City,[2] [we,] the ones most worthy of honor, will surely drive out therefrom those most contemptible ones!'..." (63:8). Upon hearing this statement, his son ʿAbd Allāh said to the Prophet, "He, by God, is the most contemptible one, and you are the one most worthy of honor, O Messenger of God! If you give me permission, I will kill him. What I fear is that you will instruct some [other] Muslim to kill him. If that happens, I will not be able to bear to see my father's slayer alive on earth, and I will kill him as well. And then I will have slain a believer for the sake of an unbeliever and will enter the hell fire!" In response the Prophet said, "Rather, let us be good companions to him and treat him with kindness. Otherwise, people will say that Muhammad kills his friends. Honor your father and be a good friend to him."

When ʿAbd Allāh's father died, he came to the Prophet and asked him to pray over him, saying, "O Messenger of God, give me your tunic for me to wrap him in, and pray for God to forgive him." The Prophet gave him his tunic, saying, "When you have finished burying him, inform me." When he was about to pray over ʿAbd Allāh ibn Ubayy, ʿUmar pulled him aside and said, "Has God not forbidden you to pray over hypocrites?" The Prophet replied, "I have been given a choice in this matter. [As God has said], '...whether thou dost pray that they be forgiven or dost not pray for them...'" (9:80), whereupon he went ahead and prayed over him. Following this God revealed the words, "And never shalt thou pray over any of them that has died, and never shalt thou stand by his grave" (9:84), after which he ceased praying over hypocrites who had died.[3]

INSTANCES OF APOSTASY DURING THE PROPHET'S LIFETIME

[THE FIRST INSTANCE]

Those who Apostatized after the Prophet's 'Night Journey and Ascension'

There is wide disagreement among historians and scholars of the Prophet's biography concerning the date of what is known as the Night Journey and Ascension. A number of them maintain that it took place during the 'year of sorrow', that is, the sixth year of the Apostle's prophetic mission, in which his paternal uncle, Abū Ṭālib and his wife Khadījah died. Others hold that it took place one year before the Hijrah.[4] In any case, the majority of historians and scholars of the Prophet's biography mention that some of the people who had earlier embraced Islam committed apostasy after the Messenger of God spoke of what had happened to him on the night he was taken on his miraculous journey from Makkah to Jerusalem. Among those who mention this are Ibn Hishām who, in his biography of the Prophet, quotes Ibn Isḥāq on the authority of al-Ḥasan who, in his hadith concerning the Prophet's night journey, states, "Most of the people said, 'That can't possibly be true. It takes one of our caravans an entire month to get from Makkah to Damascus, and another month for it to get back! So can Muhammad make the same journey and return to Makkah in a single night?' And many of those who had embraced Islam turned away from the faith."[5] However, he does not name or specify the number of those who apostatized.

Al-Ḥākim relates in *al-Mustradrak* that ʿĀ'ishah, said, "When the Prophet was taken on his night journey to the Aqsa Mosque, people began talking about this and some of those who had believed in him before turned back and took the matter to Abū Bakr."[6]

Imām Aḥmad relates in *al-Musnad* and al-Nasā'ī in *al-Sunan al-Kubrā*, on the authority of Ibn ʿAbbās, that, "The Prophet was taken on his night journey to Jerusalem, then returned on the same night and spoke to them about his journey, the distinguishing features of Jerusalem, and their caravan. In response, some people said, 'We do not believe what Muhammad is saying,' and reverted to unbelief, after which God struck their necks with Abū Jahl..."[7] That is, they later fought against the Prophet and the Muslims alongside the polytheists in the Battle of Badr, and some of them were killed.

What bears noting here is that none of the accounts that speak of the apostasy of some of those who had once believed and placed their trust in the Prophet and his message mentions specific names, nor does it specify the number of those who apostatized. Rather, they all speak of the event in an unqualified manner. Similarly, in the traditions they quote, Qur'anic commentators mention nothing of this nature in their explanations of the words of God, "And lo! We said unto thee, [O Prophet,] 'Behold, thy Sustainer encompasses all mankind [within His knowledge and might]: and so We have ordained that the vision which We have shown thee – as also the tree [of hell] cursed in this Qur'an – shall be but a trial for men. Now [by Our mentioning hell] We convey a warning to them: but [if they are bent on denying the truth,] this [warning] only increases their gross, overweening arrogance'" (17:60). The only thing mentioned in this connection is what al-Ṭabarī states on the authority of Qatādah, who, commenting on the phrase, "...and so We have ordained that the vision which We have shown thee shall be but a trial for men", states: "God showed him signs and taught him lessons on his journey to Jerusalem." Then he adds: "He related to us that when the Messenger of God spoke to them of his journey, some people apostatized after having become Muslims. Amazed, they denied that it could have happened, saying, 'Are you telling us that you made a two-month journey in a single night?!'"[8]

Al-Ṭabarī concludes his commentary on the verse: "...and so We have ordained that the vision which We have shown thee shall be but a trial for men" by stating, "That is, it was to be a trial for those who apostatized from Islam when they were informed of the vision that the Messenger of God had seen, and for the polytheists of Makkah whose hearing of what the Prophet had to say about this event caused them to go to even greater extremes in their error and unbelief."[9]

However, all of these reports are *āḥād*, or solitary hadiths,* concerning an event of such critical importance that it deserves to have been reported by a much larger number of individuals.

[THE SECOND INSTANCE]

Those who Apostatized after the Emigration to Abyssinia

ʿUbayd Allāh ibn Jaḥsh, Abū Jaḥsh

Ibn Hishām's biography of the Prophet states: "Ibn Isḥāq says, '...and as for ʿUbayd Allāh ibn Jaḥsh, he remained in a state of confusion until he embraced Islam, after which he emigrated with the Muslims to Abyssinia together with his wife Umm Ḥabībah, the daughter of Abū Sufyān, who was a Muslim. When he arrived in Abyssinia, ʿUbayd Allāh left Islam and became a Christian, and died there as a Christian. After embracing Christianity, ʿUbayd Allāh would pass by the Prophet's Companions in Abyssinia and say to them, "We have seen [the truth], whereas you are still trying to gain your sight."'"[10] Biographers and genealogists likewise report the apostasy of ʿUbayd Allāh ibn Jaḥsh and how, after entering Islam, he became a Christian in the land of Abyssinia and remained a Christian till his death.[11]

Al-Sakrān ibn ʿAmr

Al-Balādhurī writes in *Ansāb al-Ashrāf* that "al-Sakrān ibn ʿAmr emigrated to Abyssinia during the second emigration that took place to that country with his wife Sawdah Bint Zamʿah. It has also been said that he took part in both emigrations to Abyssinia, after which he came to Makkah and died before the Hijrah (that is, the emigration to Madinah), whereupon he was buried by the Messenger of God, who took Sawdah Bint Zamʿah as his wife. There are some who say that al-Sakrān ibn ʿAmr died in Abyssinia as a Muslim, while others, including Abū ʿUbaydah Maʿmar,[12] say that he came to Makkah, then returned to Abyssinia as an apostate or Christian, and died there."[13]

[THE THIRD INSTANCE]

The Apostasy of the Recorder of the Revelation

The scribe for Banū al-Najjār

Al-Bukhārī narrates on the authority of Anas that, "There was a Christian man who entered Islam and recited *Sūrah al-Baqarah* and *Sūrah Āl ʿImrān*. This man used to record for the Prophet.[14] However, he then reverted to Christianity, and would say, 'All Muhammad knows is what I've written down for him.' God then caused the man to die and they buried him. The next morning, the earth had spit him out. They said, 'This is the work of Muhammad and his Companions. They came looking for our friend after he fled from them, and threw him down here.' Then they dug the grave as deep as they could. However, the next morning, the earth had spit him out a second time. When they saw this, they realized that what had happened had not been the act of a human being, and they left him where he was."[15]

In the account narrated by Muslim one reads that, "There was among us a man from the tribe of Banū al-Najjār who had recited *Sūrah al-Baqarah* and *Sūrah Āl ʿImrān*, and who used to record for the Messenger of God. However, he then fled and joined up with the followers of earlier revelation. When he reached them, they gave him a place of honor, saying admiringly, 'This man used to record for Muhammad.' However, it wasn't long before God caused him to die in their midst."[16]

ʿAbd Allāh ibn Saʿd ibn Abī Sarḥ al-Qurashī al-ʿĀmirī

Abū Dāwūd narrates on the authority of Ibn ʿAbbās that "ʿAbd Allāh ibn Abī Sarḥ used to record for the Messenger of God. However, Satan caused him to stumble, and he joined up with the unbelievers. On the day when Makkah was conquered, the Messenger of God gave instructions that he should be put to death; however, ʿUthmān ibn ʿAffān made a plea on his behalf, in response to which the Messenger of God granted him protection."[17]

Al-Balādhurī states, "As for ʿAbd Allāh ibn Saʿd ibn Abī Sarḥ, he embraced Islam and used to record for the Messenger of God. The Messenger of God would dictate to him, *al-kāfirīn* ('those who deny the truth') and instead he would write, *al-ẓālimīn* ('the unjust'); he would dictate *ʿazīzun ḥakīm* ('All-Powerful, All-Wise'), and he would write instead, *ʿalīmun ḥakīm* ('All-Knowing, All-Wise'), and so forth. He would say, 'I speak as Muhammad speaks, and I bring forth something similar to what Muhammad brings forth,' after which God revealed the words, 'And who could be more wicked than he who invents a lie about God, or says, "This has been revealed unto me," the while nothing has been revealed to him? – or he who says, "I, too, can bestow from on high the like of what God has bestowed?"' (6:93). He then fled to Makkah as an apostate, and the Messenger of God gave instructions for him to be killed. However, ʿAbd Allāh ibn Abī Sarḥ was ʿUthmān ibn ʿAffān's brother by virtue of having suckled from the same woman, as a result of which ʿUthmān pleaded fervently on his behalf until the Messenger of God relented..."[18] However, this report conflicts with what has been reported widely, and with indubitable certainty, concerning the fact that when all verses of the Qur'an were dictated by the Prophet, those who recorded them would both write them down and recite them aloud. For if he was, in fact, changing what he wrote, was he showing what he had written to someone else? And had anyone noticed what was happening before he announced it himself? In any case, this report serves as evidence of the fact that there is no legally prescribed penalty in Islam for apostasy, since if there were, the Messenger of God would not have relented in response to ʿUthmān's intercession on this man's behalf. Rather, he would have said to him, as he had once said to Usāmah when he sought to intercede for a woman from the tribe of Banū Makhzūm who had been found guilty of stealing, "Are you asking me to change one of the limits set by God?"[19]

[THE FOURTH INSTANCE]

Those whom the Messenger of God Declared could be Killed with Impunity Due to Harm they had Caused and Crimes they had Committed along with their Apostasy

When the Messenger of God entered Makkah victoriously in the year 8 AH/629 CE, he had instructed his leading men not to kill anyone but those who had fought against the Muslims, as he wanted Makkah to be conquered peacefully. However, he did order a group of individuals, whom he named specifically, to be put to death even if they were seeking refuge under the covering of the Kaʿbah. The group included six men and four women, namely: ʿIkrimah ibn Abī Jahl, Habbār ibn al-Aswad, ʿAbd Allāh ibn Saʿd ibn Abī Sarḥ, Miqyas ibn Ṣubābah al-Laythī, al-Ḥuwayrith ibn Nuqaydh, ʿAbd Allāh ibn Hilāl ibn Khaṭal al-Adramī, Hind Bint ʿUtbah, Sārah, the servant of ʿAmr ibn Hishām, and ʿAbd Allāh ibn Khaṭal's two song-stresses, Fartanā and Quraybah, who was also known as ʿArnab.[20] The reason for this was that these individuals had incited the polytheists to go to war against the Muslims and prevent them from following in God's path. Among these there were individuals whose other crimes were associated with apostasy, including:

Miqyas ibn Ṣubābah al-Laythī

The reason the Messenger of God ordered this man killed was that he had murdered a man from among the Supporters (meaning the *Anṣār*, the Prophet's supporters in Madinah) who had killed his brother by accident, then returned to Quraysh as a polytheist.[21]

Al-Balādhurī states, "As for Miqyas ibn Ṣubābah al-Kinānī, he had a brother by the name of Hishām ibn Ṣubābah ibn Ḥazn who had become a Muslim and had taken part in the Battle of Muraysīʿ[22] with the Messenger of God, during which he was killed accidentally by one of the Supporters, who thought that Hishām was one of the polytheists. Miqyas came to the Messenger of God, who ruled that he should receive blood money from the paternal relatives of the Helper who had accidentally murdered his brother Hishām. Miqyas took the blood money and declared himself a Muslim. Thereafter, however, he assaulted the man who had killed his brother and murdered him, then fled as an apostate, saying,

> It gratifies the soul to have spent the night in the trench,
> One's robes spattered with the blood of the treacherous.

Hence, the Messenger of God gave orders to anyone who met up with him to put him to death."[23] The reason for this was that he was a murderer, someone who had broken with his nation and community, and joined enemy ranks. The sin of apostasy in this case was followed by a crime. The order given by the Messenger of God to kill Miqyas ibn Ṣubābah was not due to his apostasy; rather, it was a form of retribution for the person he had murdered.

ʿAbd Allāh ibn Khaṭal

Ibn Isḥāq states, "ʿAbd Allāh ibn Khaṭal was a man of the tribe of Banū Taym ibn Ghālib, and orders were given to kill him [on the day when Makkah was conquered]. A Muslim, he had been sent out by the Messenger of God as an alms collector, and one of the Supporters was sent out with him; he also had a Muslim servant with him. They stopped somewhere to camp and ʿAbd Allāh ibn Khaṭal instructed the servant to slaughter a billy goat and prepare him some food. He then went to sleep. When he awoke and the servant still hadn't prepared anything for him, he attacked him and killed him, then turned apostate and reverted to polytheism."[24] This man, then, was guilty of murder as well, and his apostasy was an additional offense. He was a highway robber, a thief, and someone who had behaved in an untrustworthy manner with public funds. In addition, he went to war against the Messenger of God and incited others to fight against him. ʿAbd Allāh ibn Khaṭal is mentioned by al-Balādhurī, whose account differs little from that of Ibn Isḥāq. He states:

> He embraced Islam and emigrated to Madinah, after which the Messenger of God sent him out as an alms collector. He sent with him a man from the tribe of Khuzāʿah, whom he attacked and killed.

The reason was that when ʿAbd Allāh ibn Khaṭal came one day and found that he [the man from Khuzāʿah] had not prepared any food for him, he flew into a rage and beat him to death. Then he said, "Muhammad will kill me for this," so he apostatized and fled, taking the alms that were with him. He betook himself to Makkah, saying to its people, "I have found no religion better than yours." ʿAbd Allāh ibn Khaṭal had two songstresses who used to satirize the Messenger of God in song, and the polytheists would gather with him to listen to them and drink wine. On the day when Makkah was conquered, the Messenger of God said, "Kill him even if he is clinging to the covering of the Kaʿbah," and he was killed by Abū Barazah al-Aslamī...[25]

[THE FIFTH INSTANCE]

Men from the Tribe of ʿUkal

Al-Bukhārī tells us in his *Ṣaḥīḥ*:

> It was reported to me by Qutaybah ibn Saʿīd, on the authority of Abū Bishr Ismāʿīl ibn Ibrāhīm al-Asadī, on the authority of al-Ḥajjāj ibn Abī ʿUthmān, on the authority of Abū Rajā' of the family of Abū Qilābah, on the authority of Abū Qilābah, that [Caliph] ʿUmar ibn ʿAbd al-ʿAzīz granted people permission to enter his court and said to them, "What do you say about the practice of *qasāmah*?"[26] They replied, "It is a kind of rightful reprisal, and it has been employed by some caliphs in carrying out retribution." He said to me, "And what do you say, Abū Qilābah?" He then gave me a platform from which to address the people who were gathered.
>
> I said, "O Commander of the Faithful, you have the most elite soldiers and the noblest of the Arabs [under your command]. However, if fifty of these men bore witness against a married man in Damascus that he had committed adultery though they had never seen him, would you have him stoned?" "No," he replied. Then I continued, "If fifty of these men bore witness against a man in Hims, saying that he had committed theft yet without ever having seen him, would you

> have his hand cut off?" "No," he replied. I said, "Verily, the Messenger of God never killed anyone except under one of three conditions: For murder, adultery, or apostasy from Islam which led him to wage war on the Messenger of God."
>
> The people objected, saying, "Did Anas ibn Mālik not report that the Messenger of God had people's hands cut off and their eyes put out with hot nails, after which he had them cast out into the sun to perish?" I replied, "I will tell you the hadith passed down by Anas in this regard. He says that eight men from the tribe of ʿUkal came to the Messenger of God and pledged themselves to be Muslims. However, they found the land [on which they were staying] to be unwholesome, and they fell ill. They complained of this to the Messenger of God, who said, 'Why do you not go out with our shepherd and drink some of his camels' milk ...?' 'We will do so,' they said. So they went out and drank the camels' milk ..., and recovered. However, they then murdered the Messenger of God's shepherd and drove the livestock away with them. When news of this reached the Messenger of God, he sent after them and they were brought back, whereupon he ordered that their hands and feet be cut off, that their eyes be put out with hot nails, and that they be cast out into the sun to die." ʿAnbasah ibn Saʿīd then said, "I swear, I have never heard such a thing before..."[27]

This is a solitary hadith (*ḥadīth āḥād*)* concerning an event for which there would have been every reason to make it widely known and relate it through numerous independent chains of transmission, especially given the fact that it contains mention of an exemplary punishment of this degree of seriousness. This type of account has to be documented in a manner that excludes all doubt concerning its reliability; moreover, it would have to have been circulated widely, since it describes a crime that affects what is referred to in modern parlance as 'state security'. After all, what could have been more serious than what was done by these men: apostasy from Islam, murder, theft, intimidation and stirring up strife!

It must be stressed again that this is a solitary hadith concerning an event which the Arabs, in particular, would have had every reason to relate and circulate widely. This hadith speaks of mutilation, which is something that the Messenger of God absolutely forbade. The Messenger of God was sent as a mercy to all the worlds, and his law is a law of amelioration and compassion which lays aside the shackles and undue burdens of the law that preceded it. Moreover, the Prophet would not have imposed on them a punishment that was similar to the crime they had committed, even in keeping with the law of retribution and like for like, because he had forbidden such practices.[28] As for the claim that the Prophet only forbade such practices later, it does not resolve the questions raised by the hadith. Consequently, it remains a seriously problematic hadith which calls for a thorough study of its entire chain of transmission and its content. And God knows best.

THE PHENOMENON OF HYPOCRISY

The phenomenon of hypocrisy was widespread in Madinah. Moreover, the hypocrites were known to the Messenger of God, since they had certain distinguishing characteristics and ways of expressing themselves, and tended to take certain positions on certain occasions which would expose them, revealing their dissimulation, their dishonesty, and the phoniness of the faith they professed. If we compare the hypocrite with either the declared unbeliever or the open apostate, we will find that the hypocrite poses the greatest danger by far to Islam and Muslims, both individually and collectively. The hypocrites of the Prophet's day would spread untruths that stirred up unrest and division; in addition, they engaged in terrorism, concealment, infiltration and deceit, and in some situations, inflicted considerable damage on Islam's internal front.

The Qur'an describes them in the opening verses of *Sūrah al-Baqarah*, highlighting their psychological features and showing them to be a group whose distinguishing traits need to be brought to light so as to rob them of opportunities to harm the Messenger of God and the believers. In *Sūrah Āl ʿImrān*, the Qur'an reveals an important aspect of their characters and their ways of plotting against the Messenger of God and the believers in critical situations such as the Battle of Uḥud. God Almighty declares:

> O you who have attained to faith! Be not like those who are bent on denying the truth and say of their brethren [who die] after having set out on a journey to faraway places or gone forth to war, "Had they but remained with us, they would not have died," or, "they would not have been slain" – for God will cause such thoughts to become a source of bitter regret in their hearts, since it is God who grants life and deals death. And God sees all that you do. And if indeed you are slain or die in God's cause, then surely forgiveness from God and His grace are better than all that one could amass [in this world]: for, indeed, if you die or are slain, it will surely be unto God that you shall be gathered.

> And it was by God's grace that thou [O Prophet] didst deal gently with thy followers: for if thou hadst been harsh and hard of heart, they would indeed have broken away from thee. Pardon them, then, and pray that they be forgiven. And take counsel with them in all matters of public concern; then, when thou hast decided upon a course of action, place thy trust in God: for, verily, God loves those who place their trust in Him. If God succors you, none can ever overcome you; but if He should forsake you, who could succor you thereafter? In God, then, let the believers place their trust!

> And it is not conceivable that a prophet should deceive – since he who deceives shall be faced with his deceit on the Day of Resurrection, when every human being shall be repaid in full for whatever he has done, and none shall be wronged. Is then he who strives after God's goodly acceptance like unto him who has earned the burden of God's condemnation and whose goal is hell? – and how vile a journey's end! They are on [entirely] different levels in the sight of God; for God sees all that they do.

Indeed, God bestowed a favor upon the believers when he raised up in their midst an apostle from among themselves, to convey His messages unto them, and to cause them to grow in purity, and to impart unto them the divine writ as well as wisdom – whereas before that they were indeed, most obviously, lost in error. And do you, now that a calamity has befallen you after you had inflicted twice as much [on your foes], ask yourselves, "How has this come about?" Say: "It has come from your own selves." Verily, God has the power to will anything: and all that befell you on the day when the two hosts met in battle happened by God's leave, so that He might mark out the [true] believers, and mark out those who were tainted with hypocrisy and, when they were told, "Come, fight in God's cause" – or, "Defend yourselves" – answered, "If we but knew [that it would come to a] fight, we would indeed follow you." Unto apostasy were they nearer on that day than unto faith, uttering with their mouths something which was not in their hearts, the while God knew fully well what they were trying to conceal: they who, having themselves held back [from fighting, later] said of their [slain] brethren, "Had they but paid heed to us, they would not have been slain." Say: "Avert, then, death from yourselves, if what you say is true!"

But do not think of those that have been slain in God's cause as dead. Nay, they are alive! With their Sustainer have they their sustenance, exulting in that [martyrdom] which God has bestowed upon them out of His bounty. And they rejoice in the glad tiding given to those [of their brethren] who have been left behind and have not yet joined them, that no fear need they have, and neither shall they grieve: they rejoice in the glad tiding of God's blessings and bounty, and [in the promise] that God will not fail to requite the believers who responded to the call of God and the Apostle after misfortune had befallen them.

A magnificent requital awaits those of them who have persevered in doing good and remained conscious of God: those who have been warned by other people, "Behold, a host has gathered against you; so beware of them!" – whereupon this only increased their faith, so that

> they answered, "God is enough for us; and how excellent a guardian is He!" – and returned [from the battle] with God's blessings and bounty, without having been touched by evil: for they had been striving after God's goodly acceptance – and God is limitless in His great bounty.
>
> It is but Satan who instills [into you] fear of his allies: so fear them not, but fear Me, if you are [truly] believers! (3:156–175)

Ibn Ḥazm expresses a peculiar point of view in *al-Muḥallā* when he says, "...there are those who have said that the Messenger of God knew who the hypocrites were, and that he knew that they were apostates, that is, those who had reverted to unbelief after professing Islam. The Prophet was [once] confronted by a man who accused him of making an unequal, and hence unjust, distribution among his men, which is true apostasy. Nevertheless, he did not kill him. Such people conclude from this that there is no death penalty in Islam for someone who commits apostasy, since if there were, the Messenger of God would have carried it out against the apostate hypocrites." Ibn Ḥazm goes on to say:

> We shall mention every verse according to which the Messenger of God knew the hypocrites by name, and we will show that the hypocrites belonged to one of two groups: (1) those whom he never knew about, and (2) those who were exposed, as a result of which he came to know who they were and they repented. However, the Prophet never knew whether they were sincere or insincere in their repentance. And once we have made this clear, we will have disproved the claim of those who argue that the existence of the hypocrites in the Prophet's day demonstrates that there is no death penalty in Islam for apostasy.[29]

He then proceeds to fill over forty pages with support for his assertion that the Messenger of God had no knowledge of those who were hypocrites, or that as soon as he came to know of their hypocrisy, they would flee from the consequences by repenting.

The claim being made by Ibn Ḥazm in this connection and his assertion that the Messenger of God had no knowledge of who the hypocrites were – despite the fact that many verses of the Qur'an served to acquaint the Messenger of God with them and their characteristics – is truly astonishing. Indeed, there are numerous hadiths which indicate that the Messenger of God knew the hypocrites by their distinguishing marks and their way of speaking. He used to tell Ḥudhayfah and some of his other Companions of certain individuals' hypocrisy. Moreover, supposing the Prophet was not, in fact, familiar with some of the hypocrites of his day: What about those with whom he was familiar and whom others proposed that he kill only for him to refuse, saying, "Let it not be said that Muhammad kills his friends"? When the son of the hypocrites' ringleader, Ibn Ubayy [ibn] Salūl, proposed to the Prophet that he kill his father, he said, "Rather, let us honor him and treat him with kindness."

In his assertion that the Messenger of God was ignorant of who the hypocrites were, Ibn Ḥazm was guilty of a major oversight. It is an assertion that is unacceptable from a careful thinker such as he was, and its inaccuracy should not have been lost on a scholar of his caliber. The same can be said for the oversight which he committed when he claimed that the phrase, "There shall be no coercion in matters of faith" has been abrogated, though he knew full well that this statement is classified as a report, and would, therefore, not be subject to abrogation even in the view of those who hold the notion of abrogation to be valid.[30] Moreover, even if we did acknowledge the validity of the notion of abrogation, we would not be able to accept the abrogation of part of a verse while allowing its other parts to stand. Hence, it was indeed an oversight on Ibn Ḥazm's part, and the seriousness of an oversight is measured by the stature of the person who commits it.

God commanded the Prophet to strive against the deniers of the truth and the hypocrites. But how could he have been commanded to strive against people whom he could not identify? God declares:

> O Prophet! Strive hard against the deniers of the truth and the hypocrites, and be adamant with them. And [if they do not repent,] their

> goal shall be hell – and how vile a journey's end! [The hypocrites] swear by God that they have said nothing [wrong]; yet most certainly have they uttered a saying which amounts to a denial of the truth, and have [thus] denied the truth after [having professed] their self-surrender to God: for they were aiming at something which was beyond their reach. And they could find no fault [with the Faith] save that God had enriched them and [caused] His Apostle [to enrich them] out of His bounty! Hence, if they repent, it will be for their own good; but if they turn away, God will cause them to suffer grievous suffering in this world and in the life to come, and they will find no helper on earth, and none to give [them] succor. (9:73–74)[31]

The verses following these two complement their meaning and shed light on the hypocrites in such a way that it would be difficult to claim that they were unknown to the Prophet. *Sūrah al-Munāfiqūn*, the eighteenth surah of the Qur'an to be revealed in Madinah says:

> When the hypocrites come unto thee, they say, "We bear witness that thou art indeed God's Apostle!" But God knows that thou art truly His Apostle; and He bears witness that the hypocrites are indeed false [in their declaration of faith].
>
> They have made their oaths a cover [for their falseness], and thus they turn others away from the path of God. Evil, indeed, is all that they are wont to do: this, because [they profess that] they have attained to faith, whereas [inwardly] they deny the truth; and so, a seal has been set on their hearts, so that they can no longer understand [what is true and what is false].
>
> Now when thou seest them, their outward appearance may please thee; and when they speak, thou art inclined to lend ear to what they say. [But though they may seem as sure of themselves] as if they were timbers [firmly] propped up, they think that every shout is [directed] against them. They are the [real] enemies [of all faith], so beware of them. [They deserve the imprecation,], "May God destroy them!"

> How perverted are their minds! – for, when they are told, "Come, the Apostle of God will pray [unto God] that you be forgiven," they turn their heads away, and thou canst see how they draw back in their false pride. As for them, it is all the same whether thou dost pray that they be forgiven or dost not pray for them: God will not forgive them – for, behold, God does not bestow His guidance upon such iniquitous folk.
>
> It is they who say [to their compatriots], "Do not spend anything on those who are with God's Apostle, so that they [may be forced to] leave." However, unto God belong the treasures of the heavens and the earth: but this truth the hypocrites cannot grasp.
>
> [And] they say, "Indeed, when we return to the City, [we,] the ones most worthy of honor, will surely drive out therefrom those most contemptible ones!" However, all honor belongs to God, and [thus] to His Apostle and those who believe [in God]: but of this the hypocrites are not aware. (63:1–8)

After reading these verses, one could not possibly say that the reason the Messenger of God did not kill the hypocrites was that he did not know who they were. On the contrary, even individuals among the Companions knew their names, their family lineages, and their way of plotting to do harm to Islam and the Muslims. God states explicitly that "they are the [real] enemies [of all faith], so beware of them." Given that God has stated this so clearly and warned against them so sternly, how could it be said after this that the Prophet did not know who they were?

ʿAbd Allāh ibn Ubayy and those who falsely accused ʿĀ'ishah were known for their hostility to Islam and the Muslims. Al-Bukhārī, with the chain of transmission which he provides, relates that after ʿAbd Allāh ibn Ubayy had uttered his infamous words, "Indeed, when we return to the City [Madinah] [we,] the ones most worthy of honor, will surely drive out therefrom those most contemptible ones!", ʿUmar rose and said, "O Messenger of God, allow me to kill this hypocrite." In response, the Prophet said to him, "Leave him alone. Let it not be said that Muhammad kills his friends." In his commentary on the Qur'an, Ibn Kathīr narrates a similar account which conveys the same meaning. Ibn Kathīr's account tells us that after returning to Madinah, the Prophet said to ʿUmar, "Truly I tell you, if you had killed him on that day, you would have unduly given offense to men who, if I instructed them to kill him now, would kill him [without hesitation],[32] and people would have said that I fall on my friends and imprison them in order to put them to death."[33]

It will be clear from the foregoing that there is no divinely revealed punishment in accordance with which everyone who reverts to unbelief after having believed is to be put to death. In neither the Qur'an nor the actions of the Prophet will we find any indication that he was aware that God had laid down a prescribed penalty for apostasy. For if he had been aware of such a penalty, he would not have hesitated to carry it out. Indeed, it was the Prophet himself who declared in connection with a case of theft that intercession is of no avail in cases involving divinely revealed penalties, and he swore that even if his daughter Fāṭimah were guilty of stealing, he would carry out the penalty and cut off her hand![34]

Scholars agree that no part of the Sunnah which speaks of a punishment that involves taking life or doing harm to a member of the human body is to be relied upon unless it is a clarification of the manner in which a punishment mentioned in the Qur'an itself is to be carried out. The reason for this is that there are innumerable, definitive passages from the Qur'an which stress the vital necessity of preserving human life and the soundness of the human body. Such texts cannot be outweighed by some other text from the Qur'an or the Sunnah, and in fact, no conflicting text exists in the first place. Moreover, the Prophet's task was to deliver, clarify, and obey the revealed message he had received in the form of the Qur'an.

When Muslim jurists saw that the Qur'an contains nothing that could be viewed as a legally prescribed punishment for apostasy, that the Sunnah – including both the Prophet's words and his actions – is likewise devoid of any such penalty, and that the freedom to choose what one will believe is a supreme value of Islam set forth in nearly two hundred verses of the Qur'an, they supported their claim that the apostate must be put to death – which they viewed as resting on a consensus [of the Prophet's Companions] – by resorting to an incompletely transmitted hadith* concerning a statement attributed to the Prophet and a number of traditions (*āthār*),* not one of which is free of questionable elements.

THE CONDITIONS SET DOWN IN THE TRUCE OF ḤUDAYBIYYAH

The Truce of Ḥudaybiyyah, which was concluded by the Messenger of God with the Qurayshites late in the year 6 AH/627 CE, stipulates the following conditions:

> This is what has been agreed upon by Muhammad ibn ʿAbd Allāh and Suhayl ibn ʿAmr. The two [parties to this treaty] agree to cease engaging in warfare against one another for a period of ten years. During this period of time, people will be free of the threat of hostilities, and will leave one another in peace. If anyone comes to Muhammad from the Qurayshite camp without the permission of his superiors, he [Muhammad] will send him back; however, if any of those who are with Muhammad comes to the Qurayshite camp, the Qurayshites will not send him back. No harm shall be done by either side to the other. Nor shall there be any theft, bribery, or treachery between us. Whoever wishes to enter into this covenant and pact on the side of Muhammad, let him do so, and whoever wishes to enter it on the side of Quraysh, let him do so.[35]

Ibn Saʿd adds in *al-Ṭabaqāt al-Kubrā*, "Muhammad will withdraw from us this year with his Companions. Thereafter he will enter [Makkah] with his Companions and remain for three days and nights. However, when they enter, they will do so bearing no arms but those carried by a traveler, and their swords shall remain in their scabbards."[36]

What bears noting here is that the conditions set forth in the treaty include an article which stipulates that "If anyone comes to Muhammad from the Qurayshite camp without the permission of his superiors, he [Muhammad] will send him back, but if any of those who are with Muhammad comes to the Qurayshite camp, they [the Qurayshites] will not send him back." No sooner had the ink dried on the treaty than a man by the name of Abū Jandal ibn Suhayl ibn ʿAmr approached the Muslims' camp, fleeing from Makkah as a convert to Islam. However, the Messenger of God declined to receive him after having signed the truce agreement with the Qurayshites. Among the things he said to Abū Jandal was, "Abū Jandal, bear up patiently and have faith in the reward you will receive from God. For indeed, God will grant you and the oppressed who are with you relief and a way out of your predicament. As for us, we have agreed to a truce with the people of Quraysh. We gave them our word and they gave us theirs with God as our witness, and we will not betray them."[37]

This conduct on the Prophet's part was a concrete demonstration of the seriousness of his and the Muslims' commitment to what was stated in the first half of the aforementioned article of the treaty agreement, even if this came at the expense of a group who had placed their faith in God and His Apostle and who wanted to join the ranks of the Muslims in Madinah. The Messenger of God indicated that these oppressed Muslims and others like them should flee with their new-found faith to some place outside Madinah as had happened with Abū Baṣīr ʿUtbah ibn Asīd, who encamped in al-ʿĪṣ in the direction of Dhū al-Marwah along the coastal road. Thereafter, people of Makkah who had embraced Islam and who were being oppressed began following him to his encampment until a group of nearly seventy men had formed.[38]

At the same time – and this is the point of greatest relevance here – the Prophet included a condition in the second half of this article from which it may be understood implicitly that he was agreeing to leave in peace those who had apostatized from Islam and who wished to join the polytheists of Quraysh without pursuing them in any way. This fact might be difficult to understand for someone who believes that it is Muslims' duty to put the apostate to death since, by agreeing to allow those who had apostatized from Islam to return to Quraysh without carrying out the legally prescribed punishment for this offense, he appeared to be neglecting to carry out a ruling which was thought to be among Islam's divinely revealed punishments. Yet God forbid that the Apostle should have agreed to sign an agreement that entailed disregard for the limits set by God!

What makes the matter even more serious is that this pact took the form of a documented political treaty which was to remain in effect for ten entire years. No Muslim who believes in the prophetic mission of Muhammad could possibly accept the notion that the Prophet wanted to achieve political or propagandistic gains in return for abandoning his commitment to carrying out one of the punishments prescribed by God Himself. Someone might claim that the Truce of Ḥudaybiyyah was signed before the time when the legally prescribed punishment for apostasy was instituted. However, this claim will backfire on those who make it, since there is no clear historical evidence to indicate the time at which this punishment was legislated, or even that it was legislated at all. In any case, the answer to this question lies in the verdict of Islamic law itself on those who apostatize from Islam, which will become apparent to readers as this discussion proceeds, God willing.

It might be claimed here that the Messenger of God did not agree to this. Rather, what was meant by agreeing to this condition was that if someone fled as an apostate from the Muslim camp to that of the Qurayshites, the Messenger of God would not be free to demand the person's return in order to carry out the punishment for apostasy. This claim would be acceptable if the text of the treaty supported it. However, it does not. For what the treaty says is, "if any of those who are with Muhammad comes to the Qurayshite camp, they [the Qurayshites] will not send him back." The text of the agreement does not specify the way in which such a person was to have come to the Qurayshite camp. Hence, it may be interpreted as referring to someone's leaving for the Qurayshite camp in a public, open fashion, just as it may be interpreted as referring to someone's fleeing in secret. Be that as it may, if the Prophet had confined those who had apostatized from Islam and wanted to defect to the Qurayshites, he would have been in violation of the covenant and its associated conditions.

DID THE MESSENGER OF GOD EVER PUT AN APOSTATE TO DEATH?

It is an established fact that never in his entire life did the Prophet put an apostate to death. Al-Shāfiʿī states:

> Never did the Prophet fail to respect the bounds set by God in relation to anyone who lived in his day. In fact, he was the most steadfast of all people in observing the limits which God had imposed on him. Hence, speaking of a woman who had committed theft and on whose behalf someone had made intercession, he said, "The reason that those who came before you were caused to perish was that if a person among them of noble lineage committed theft, he went unpunished, but if someone of lowly standing committed the same crime, the punishment would be carried out against him."

Al-Shāfiʿī adds, "Some people believed, then committed apostasy, then professed belief again. However, the Messenger of God did not put them to death." Al-Bayhaqī writes:

> We related this concerning ʿAbd Allāh ibn Abī al-Sarḥ when Satan caused him to stumble and he went and joined the unbelievers, then returned to Islam. We have also related it in connection with one of the Supporters.[39]

This negates the existence of any factual evidence that the Messenger of God killed anyone for the crime of apostasy at any time in his life. As we have noted, if he had known that he had been commanded to kill those who apostatized from his religion and that this was a ruling from God, he would not have hesitated to carry out this ruling for any reason whatsoever. As for the instances which I have cited above and which involved the killing of apostates, these were instances in which apostasy was coupled with numerous other crimes, as I have likewise mentioned. In cases such as these, apostasy was tantamount to a declaration of rebellion against the community and of enmity toward it.

Ibn al-Ṭallāʿ tells us in his *Aḥkām*, "It is not mentioned in any of the well-known [Islamic] writings that he killed an apostate or unbeliever."[40]

4

RESPONSE TO APOSTASY IN THE VERBAL SUNNAH

STATEMENTS BY THE PROPHET

In the previous chapter, the instances of apostasy which took place in the era of the Prophet and how he dealt with each of these cases were discussed. From this review it became clear that, as stated by al-Shāfiʿī, the Prophet never once killed an apostate in his entire life. We also saw that none of the well-known Islamic written works makes any mention of the Prophet's having put to death either an apostate or an unbeliever.[1]

As for the statements attributed to the Prophet, one finds solitary hadiths which contain the command to kill the apostate. One of the most salient hadiths of this type and the most widely cited among Muslim jurists, most of whom have relied on this specific hadith in arguing for the death penalty for apostates, is the one which states, "If anyone changes his religion, put him to death." This hadith became widely known after the early days of Islam. Before that time, however, it had been nothing but a solitary hadith (*ḥadīth āḥād*) which was considered to be incompletely transmitted as well as (*mursal*).*

This study suggests a link between the aforementioned hadith and the then Jewish community's attitude towards the Muslims, which is supported by a hadith handed down on the authority of Muʿādh ibn Jabal. Aḥmad relates in his *Musnad* (5:231)[2] that Muʿādh ibn Jabal came to see Abū Mūsā in Yemen, and there was a man with him.

"'Who is this?' [asked Muʿādh]. Abū Mūsā replied, 'He is a man who was a Jew, then embraced Islam, then reverted to Judaism. We have been trying to get him to return to Islam for (or so he estimated) two months.' In response, Muᶜādh said, 'I swear to God, I will not rest until you have beheaded him!' The man was then beheaded. And he [Muᶜādh] said, 'God and His Apostle have decreed: "If anyone reverts from his religion (or, whoever changes his religion), put him to death."'"

This hadith, whose chain of transmission is sound according to the criteria set down by Muslim and al-Bukhārī,[3] can be seen to be closely linked to the words of God Almighty in the Qur'an, "A section of the People of the Book say, 'Believe in the morning what is revealed to the Believers, but reject it at the end of the day; [perchance] they may [themselves] turn back.'" This man was among those who thus conspired to turn the Muslims back from their faith. Even so, he had been given an opportunity over a period of two months to repent of his crime.

This account serves as a clarification of the verse from *Sūrah Āl ᶜImrān* quoted above, and it is in light of this account that all valid chains of narrators associated with the hadith, "If anyone changes his religion, put him to death" are to be seen. In so saying, this study rejects the confused story which has been attributed to Imam ᶜAlī, and which we shall have occasion to discuss in detail below, as a basis for interpreting the aforementioned hadith. The reason for this is that Kaᶜb ibn al-Ashraf, Mālik ibn al-Ṣayf and other Jewish leaders had tried every means at their disposal to undermine the Revelation and the Prophet, but had failed to do harm to either of them. Moreover, they realized that some Jewish scholars and rabbis were holding discussions about the delegation of seventy Jews whom Moses had chosen to gather with him when he met with his Lord on the mountain, namely, the gathering recounted in the verses from *Sūrah al-Aᶜrāf*:

> And Moses chose out of his people seventy men to come [and pray for forgiveness] at a time set by Us. Then, when violent trembling seized them, he prayed: "O my Sustainer! Hadst Thou so willed, Thou wouldst have destroyed them ere this, and me [with them]. Wilt Thou destroy us for what the weak-minded among us have

done? [All] this is but a trial from Thee, whereby Thou allowest to go astray whom Thou willest, and guidest aright whom Thou willest. Thou art near unto us: grant us, then, forgiveness and have mercy on us – for Thou art the best of all forgivers! And ordain Thou for us what is good in this world as well as in the life to come: Behold, unto Thee have we turned in repentance!"

[God] answered: "With My chastisement do I afflict whom I will – but My grace overspreads everything: and so I shall confer it on those who are conscious of Me and spend in charity, and who believe in Our messages – those who shall follow the [last] Apostle, the unlettered Prophet, whom they shall find described in the Torah that is with them, and [later on] in the Gospel: [the Prophet] who will enjoin upon them the doing of what is right and make lawful to them the good things of life and forbid them the bad things, and lift from them their burdens and the shackles that were upon them [aforetime]. Those, therefore, who shall believe in him, and honor him, and succor him, and follow the light that has been bestowed from on high through him – it is they, they that shall attain to a happy state."

Say, [O Muhammad]: "O mankind! Verily, I am an apostle of God to all of you, [sent by Him] unto whom the dominion over the heavens and the earth belongs! There is no deity save Him: He [alone] grants life and deals death!" (7:155–158)

As seen earlier, it was on this occasion that Moses asked God to ease the burdens of the divinely revealed law for the children of Israel and to abrogate the ordinances that were marked by exemplary punishment, burdens and restrictions, in order that the children of Israel might be able to abide by the law more successfully. However, God's reply was to declare that the amelioration of the law's demands would be associated with an entirely new order. God declared that this new order would be distinct from that which had been associated with the law of the children of Israel – a law that had been based on exceptional, supernatural provision, nine clear signs, a supernatural punishment [of Pharaoh and his armies], and a theocracy on a holy land over a chosen people – and that those who wished to benefit from the law of amelioration and mercy would have to wait for the final Prophet with his order founded upon the seal of prophethood and the authority of the Holy Book as the supreme sign of his conclusive prophetic mission.

Hence, these Jewish leaders began trying to anticipate events. In so doing, they sought to affirm the need for Jews to remain committed to their own religion, to resist any temptation to turn away from it, and to disregard the good tidings contained in the Torah concerning the final prophet to come. At the same time, they began working to harm the Prophet and his mission in every way they possibly could:

> It is the wish of a section of the People of the Book to lead you astray. But they shall lead astray [not you], but themselves. And they do not perceive! Ye People of the Book! Why reject ye the Signs of God, of which ye are [yourselves] witnesses? Ye People of the Book! Why do ye clothe truth with falsehood, and conceal the truth, while ye have knowledge? A section of the People of the Book say: "Believe in the morning what is revealed to the Believers, but reject it at the end of the day; perchance they may [themselves] turn back. And believe no one unless he follows your religion." Say: "True guidance is the guidance of God: [Fear ye] lest a revelation be sent to someone [else] like unto that which was sent unto you? Or that those [receiving such revelation] should engage you in argument before your Lord?" Say: "All bounties are in the hand of God. He granteth them to whom He pleaseth; and God careth for all, and He knoweth all things." For His Mercy He specially chooseth whom He pleaseth; for God is the Lord of bounties unbounded. (3:69–74)[4]

Hence, if the Messenger of God ordered the execution of those who changed their religion in order to destroy Islam's inner front – by shaking Muslims' faith, especially those who were still new to Islam, by spreading falsehoods in Madinah with the aim of stirring up divisions, and by plotting the Muslims' downfall – this can only be viewed as a security issue and therefore justified. After all, there is no nation on earth that will allow others to harm it in this way. Moreover, if the Jew who was being commanded by those plotting against Islam to appear to enter Islam at the beginning of the day, then repudiate it at the end of the day realized that he would not be able to exit from Islam with the same ease with which he had entered it, he would think twice, nay a thousand times, before throwing in his lot with such conspirators. It was these schemers about whom God Almighty declared:

> Thus it is: If the hypocrites, and they in whose hearts is disease, and they who, by spreading false rumors, would cause disturbances in the City [of the Prophet] desist not [from their hostile doings], We shall indeed give thee mastery over them, [O Muhammad] – and then they will not remain thy neighbors in this [city] for more than a little while: bereft of God's grace, they shall be seized wherever they may be found, and slain one and all. Such has been God's way with those who [sinned in like manner and] passed away aforetime – and never wilt thou find any change in God's way! (33:60–62)

These verses from the Qur'an were revealed to put a stop to this type of conspiracy against Islam's internal front and attempts to rend it asunder. Hence, if the hadith according to which the Apostle said, "If anyone changes his religion, put him to death" is sound, he will have had this serious security situation in mind when he uttered the words in question. After all, as has been mentioned, it is an established, widely recognized fact that never once did the Prophet put an apostate to death simply for the act of exiting Islam. Al-Shāfiʿī states, "Some people believed, then committed apostasy, then professed belief again. However, the Messenger of God did not put them to death." Al-Bayhaqī writes:

> We related this concerning ʿAbd Allāh ibn Abī al-Sarḥ when Satan caused him to stumble and he went and joined the unbelievers, then returned to Islam. We have also related it in connection with one of the Supporters.[5]

THE HARM CAUSED BY GIVING HADITHS PRIORITY OVER THE QUR'AN

One of the most pernicious habits into which people have fallen in relation to our Islamic jurisprudence is that of placing the Hadith, at least on the level of practice, above that which is stated explicitly by the Qur'an. In so doing, they have elevated the Hadith from the status of that which clarifies and explicates the Qur'an – that which clarifies being subordinate to that which is clarified – to the status of that which is equal or parallel to the Qur'an. The end result of this process, not surprisingly, has been to allow hadiths to reign supreme over the Qur'an and pass judgment on it. As al-Awzāʿī has been quoted as saying, "The Sunnah stands in judgment over the Book."[6]

For this reason this study has considered it best to quote the hadith as it has been passed down to us with all of its varied chains of narrators and in all its different versions, as well as textual evidence in support of it and what scholars have had to say about it. In so doing, one will be able to see how scholars have put it to use, bringing it out of the realm of that which merely explicates the Qur'an and into the realm of that which rules over it and issues verdicts which are not found in the Qur'an itself. One finds, for example, that this hadith implies approval of the destruction of human life – the human life which the Qur'an takes great care to preserve and safeguard, and whose destruction it seeks to prevent by all means possible. The Qur'an is loathe to rule that human life must be taken unless there is clear evidence for the need to do so – evidence which is definitive both in terms of its meaning and in terms of the channels through which it has been passed down to us.

It should be noted that the unconditional application of this hadith leads to a result that no one would ever advocate, namely, the abrogation or suspension of nearly two hundred verses of the Qur'an which reject the principle of coercion in matters of faith and stipulate absolute human freedom to choose what one will believe and what religion one will profess! As has been seen, the Qur'an affirms that there is no earthly penalty whatsoever for the decision to change one's religion (so long as the individual concerned is not guilty of some other crime). On the contrary, what the Qur'an affirms is that the right to declare the penalty for simple apostasy (that is, apostasy not associated with any other crime) belongs to God alone. This is, in fact, God's first claim on His servants, and the injustice entailed by the act of turning away from faith is an injustice which the apostate commits against God Himself: "Do not ascribe divine powers to aught beside God; for behold, such a [false] ascribing of divinity is indeed an awesome wrong!" (31:13). Hence, it is God alone who will requite those who turn away from faith in Him.

STATEMENTS BY THE PROPHET: TRADITIONS INVOLVING ᶜUMAR IBN AL-KHAṬṬĀB

[ONE]: Mālik relates in *al-Muwaṭṭa'* (2:211)[7], that "ᶜUmar ibn al-Khaṭṭāb was approached by a man who had come from Abū Mūsā al-Ashᶜarī. ᶜUmar asked him about the people and he informed him. ᶜUmar said to him, 'Have there been any new developments?' 'Yes,' he replied, 'there is a man who reverted to unbelief after becoming a Muslim.' 'And what did you do to him?' ᶜUmar asked. 'We brought him in,' he replied, 'and beheaded him.' 'Why did you not imprison him for three days,' ᶜUmar asked, 'giving him a loaf of bread to eat every day and urging him to repent in the hope that he might return to God?!' Then ᶜUmar added, 'O God, I was not present, I gave no instructions [in this matter], and I did not express my approval when news [of it] reached me!'"

[TWO]: In *al-Tamhīd* (5:307), Ibn ᶜAbd al-Barr relates a different version of the same hadith[8] saying that "ᶜUmar was approached by a delegation from the people of Basra, who informed him that Tustur had been conquered. ᶜUmar praised God when he heard the news. Then he asked, 'Have there been any significant developments among you?' 'No, not at all, O Commander of the Faithful,' they replied, 'except for a man who turned back from his religion, and whom we killed.' 'Woe be to you!' ᶜUmar replied. 'Could you not have confined him for three days and thrown him some bread every day? Then if he had repented, you should have accepted his repentance, and if he had remained in his unbelief, you would have exempted yourselves from responsibility for him. O God, I did not witness this event, I did not command that this act be carried out, nor did I express my approval when news of it reached me!'"

[THREE]: Al-Bayhaqī (8:207) relates[9] [Anas spoke of] his coming to see ʿUmar ibn al-Khaṭṭāb, who asked, "Anas, what happened to the group of six from [the tribe of] Bakr ibn Wā'il who apostatized from Islam and joined up with the polytheists?" [Anas said], "Then I changed the subject in order to distract him from these men." But ʿUmar asked again, "What happened to the six men from [the tribe of] Bakr ibn Wā'il who apostatized from Islam and joined up with the polytheists?" "O Commander of the Faithful," replied Anas, "they were killed in the battle." "We belong to God, and to God shall we return," said ʿUmar. Then he added, "To have taken them peacefully would have been more precious to me than all the gold and silver I have now won." "But were they not bound to die?" asked Anas. "Yes, they were," he replied. "But I would have proposed that they return to Islam, and if they had refused, I would have put them in prison." In *al-Tamhīd* (5:307–308), Ibn ʿAbd al-Barr concludes his chain of transmission for this hadith with Dāwūd ibn Abī Hind. The version of the hadith related by Ibn ʿAbd al-Barr begins by saying that a group of men from [the tribe of] Bakr ibn Wā'il apostatized from Islam during the battle of Tustur. It also includes the following: "I [Anas] asked, 'And were they not bound to die? After all, they had turned away from Islam and joined the polytheists.' He [ʿUmar] replied, 'I would have proposed that they enter the door through which they had exited. If they had agreed to do so, I would have accepted their repentance, and if they had refused, I would have kept them in prison.'"

[FOUR]: Ibn Ḥazm (13:124) writes that they were informed[10] that Abū Mūsā al-Ashʿarī had killed Juḥaynah the Liar and his companions.[11] Anas states, "So I came to ʿUmar," after which he relates an account similar to the account related above by al-Bayhaqī.

Such accounts should serve to explain one another.

PROBLEMS ASSOCIATED WITH THE HADITH

As will be seen, when one views this hadith in light of Qur'anic verses whose meanings are definitive and clear, it presents no difficulty. However, when the various versions of the hadith are cited in isolation from the Qur'an, and when some narrators connect these accounts with other events and stories, the hadith may become incomprehensible. In addition, as noted earlier, problems have been noted by hadith scholars in relation to its chains of narrators, chains of transmission, and content. The hadith has been handed down on the authority of Ibn ʿAbbās and ʿĀ'ishah, Muʿādh ibn Jabal, Abū Hurayrah, ʿIṣmah ibn Mālik al-Khaṭmī and ʿAbd Allāh ibn ʿUmar. However, the stories in the context of which the hadith has been related vary widely. As related on the authority of Ibn ʿAbbās, the hadith has been passed down through two chains of narrators: (1) the one that begins with ʿIkrimah, and (2) the one that begins with Anas ibn Mālik. As for the version passed down through ʿIkrimah, it turns on a narrator by the name of Ayyūb ibn Abī Tamīmah al-Sikhtiyānī, through whom the hadith gained wide circulation. It was on the authority of Ayyūb ibn Abī Tamīmah al-Sikhtiyānī that the hadith was then narrated by the following ten individuals: (1) Ḥammād ibn Zayd, (2) Sufyān ibn ʿUyyaynah, (3) ʿAbd al-Wārith ibn Saʿīd, (4) Wuhayb ibn Khālid, (5) Maʿmar ibn Rāshid, (6) Saʿīd ibn Iyyās al-Jarīrī, (7) Saʿīd ibn Abī ʿUrūbah, (8) ʿAbd al-Wahhāb ibn ʿAbd al-Majīd al-Thaqafī, (9) Jarīr ibn Ḥāzim, and (10) Ismāʿīl ibn Ibrāhīm ibn ʿUlayyah. The fact that all of these are reliable narrators does not prevent the hadith from being a solitary hadith (*ḥadīth āḥād*) and, indeed, an incompletely transmitted one (*mursal*), as has been pointed out earlier. The reason for this is that a hadith cannot be characterized by unquestionable reliability (*tawātur*),* acceptability to the Muslim community at large (*istifāḍah*),* or wide circulation (*ishtihār*) if it only gained circulation after the era of the Companions who narrated it.

As has been noted, the hadith has been narrated with an incomplete chain of transmission, while some of its chains of narrators contain instances of concealing *(tadlīs)*,* and this despite the fact that narrators differ widely in their accounts of the incident referred to. One of them, for example, states that the Caliph ʿAlī ibn Abī Ṭālib first gave orders that a group of apostates or unbelievers should be killed, after which he cast their corpses into the fire, while another states that he gave orders that they should be exposed to smoke from the fire in the hope that they would repent. However, an event of this magnitude is one that would have to have been witnessed by thousands, and accounts of which would have to have been related by thousands as well, especially in view of the fact that just as ʿAlī, Commander of the Faithful, had supporters and helpers, so also did he have numerous enemies and opponents who, if this account is true, could have exploited it as a way of discrediting ʿAli, using it as a basis on which to accuse him of having claimed divinity for himself because he had inflicted a chastisement on others like that which God will inflict on human beings in the afterlife. But how could he have made such a claim given the accounts according to which the person closest to him – his cousin ʿAbd Allāh ibn ʿAbbās – sought to correct him?

This hadith has been related by chains of narrators some of which have been declared sound by some hadith scholars, some of which have been found to be incomplete, with missing and/or anonymous narrators, some of which involve *tadlīs*, and some of which are confused and inconsistent (*muḍṭarib*).* However, such phenomena are not acceptable in relation to an event as momentous as this one, the likes of which had not occurred in the eras of those who had preceded ʿAlī, nor was any like it to take place in the eras of those who succeeded him.

According to one account, those who were burned to death by the Caliph ʿAlī were *zanādiqah*,[12] whereas according to other versions they belonged to a national group referred to as the Zuṭṭ.[13] According to other versions, they had taken an idol into the home of one of them and begun to worship it, and when the Commander of the Faithful was informed of the matter, he went to them. They brought out a marble statue to him, and he gave orders for the house to be burned down over their heads.

The story also appears in a form according to which a group of people came to the Commander of the Faithful and stood at the mosque door saying, "ᶜAlī is our Lord." ᶜAlī went out to them and said, "Woe be to you! What are you saying?" "You are He," they replied. "You are our Lord, our Creator, our Sustainer." He said to them, "Woe to you. I am nothing but a creature like you!" etc.

Then the story says that he let them go free, asking them to mend their ways and to return to him the next day repentant. However, they did not repent, and he gave them a third day. He then dug a trench for them. It is said that he beheaded them, then threw them into the trench to burn their dead bodies. This account contains no mention of how many individuals were involved, nor anything about their affiliations or the countries or tribes from which they came. However, such omissions would have been highly unusual in that era even in relation to incidents of far less importance than this one, assuming that it actually took place. More will follow on this topic in the proper place.

THE HADITH AND THE CHAINS OF ITS NARRATORS

Let us begin with what was said by Ibn ᶜAbd al-Barr[14] concerning this hadith. He states, "There is no disagreement over the death penalty for apostasy. Nor is there any inconsistency on this point among the accounts narrated on the authority of the Prophet and the Sunnah" (*al-Tamhīd*, 5:318). This is a generalization which calls for careful examination, especially given what we know now, and will come to see below, concerning what has been said about this hadith.

According to al-Zaylaᶜī, a Ḥanafī, this hadith was narrated based on accounts passed down on the authority of Ibn ᶜAbbās, Muᶜāwiyah ibn Ḥaydah, and ᶜĀ'ishah (*Naṣb al-Rāyah*, 3:456). It has, in addition, been narrated based on accounts passed down on the authority of Muᶜādh ibn Jabal, Abū Hurayrah, ᶜIṣmah ibn Mālik al-Khaṭmī, and ᶜAbd Allāh ibn ᶜUmar. It has also been narrated with an incomplete chain of transmission based on accounts passed down on the authority of al-Ḥasan and Zayd ibn Aslam.

As seen earlier, the hadith has been narrated on the authority of Ibn ʿAbbās through two different chains of narrators, one of which passes through ʿIkrimah, and the other through Anas ibn Mālik. The chain of narrators which passes through ʿIkrimah turns on Ayyūb ibn Abī al-Sikhtiyānī, through whom the hadith gained wide circulation. Moreover, the account passed down through the ʿIkrimah-Ayyūb chain agrees with that of Qatādah ibn Diʿāmah and al-Ḥakam ibn Abān, assuming that the latters' accounts are sound and trustworthy. As for the chain of narrators that passes through Anas ibn Mālik, it also turns on Qatādah ibn Diʿāmah, through whom the hadith gained wide circulation.

Ibn ʿAbd al-Barr states, "This hadith is well-known and sound; it also has a sound chain of transmission, being based on the account passed down on the authority of Ibn ʿAbbās" (*al-Tamhīd*, 5:304). In fact, for these assertions by Ibn ʿAbd al-Barr, this study finds no justification other than the fact that the hadith supports his point of view on the question!

In what follows, this hadith is shown to turn on a single narrator on whose authority it was narrated by a group, after which it spread and gained wide circulation; in the process, however, some of its difficulties were forgotten or ignored.

(1) *ʿIkrimah*: This chain, as seen earlier, begins with ʿIkrimah on the authority of Ibn ʿAbbās, and it turns on Ayyūb ibn Abī Tamīmah al-Sikhtiyānī, who gave the hadith wide circulation and on whose authority ten other individuals passed the hadith on to others.

A slave who belonged to Ibn ʿAbbās, ʿIkrimah would listen to Ibn ʿAbbās and pass on to others both things Ibn ʿAbbās had said but also things he had not said, particularly in connection with Qur'anic interpretation. ʿIkrimah remained a slave to Ibn ʿAbbās until the latter's death, at which time he was inherited by Ibn ʿAbbās's sons, who either sold him or freed him. ʿAlī ibn ʿAbd Allāh ibn ʿAbbās accused ʿIkrimah of lying about his father and bound him hand and foot, then confined him at the door to the public lavatory. When asked about this, ʿAlī replied, "This malicious man lies about my father." ʿIkrimah's reliability was challenged by Ibn Sīrīn, who also called him a liar. Speaking of ʿIkrimah, Ibn Abī Dhi'b said, "People do not cite his hadiths as evidence in support of their arguments, and they speak of him [in a manner which casts doubt on his trustworthiness]." Saʿīd ibn Jubayr said concerning ʿIkrimah, "On ʿIkrimah's authority you [people] narrate hadiths which, if I were present with him, he himself would not narrate." Similarly, Saʿīd ibn al-Musayyab used to be wary of him and warn others against him, saying, "Sooner or later, this servant of Ibn ʿAbbās's is going to be led about with a rope around his neck." This same Saʿīd would often say to his own servant, Burd, "Do not lie about me the way ʿIkrimah lied about Ibn ʿAbbās." And Ibn ʿUmar used to say the same thing to his slave Nāfiʿ.

Al-Bukhārī was criticized for narrating hadiths on the authority of ʿIkrimah, and Ibn al-Ṣalāḥ states that "...al-Bukhārī cited [hadiths narrated by] a group of narrators whose reliability had previously been challenged, including ʿIkrimah, Ibn ʿAbbās's slave." Muslim used to avoid narrating hadiths on the authority of ʿIkrimah alone, while according to Aḥmad ibn Ḥanbal, Mālik refrained from narrating any more than a single hadith on his authority. In fact, Mālik did not like ʿIkrimah to be mentioned.[15]

Ayyūb al-Sikhtiyānī (Abū Bakr ibn Tamīmah), who passed this hadith down to others from ʿIkrimah, was a man well known for his asceticism and otherworldliness, and who held ʿIkrimah in high regard and defended him untiringly. The question is: Was Ayyūb al-Sikhtiyānī's defense of ʿIkrimah attributable to his own piety and renunciation of the world? Was it an unwillingness to stoop to the practice of impugning others' reliability that lay behind this attitude on his part? The difficulty in this case lies in the fact that the hadith of concern deals not with virtuous action and the like but, rather, with the shedding of blood. So how could this pious ascetic have justified to himself the relating of this hadith on the authority of a man who was the object of suspicion, and whose reliability had been impugned by scholars of weight and influence? Whatever the answers to such questions, the fact remains that it may well have been Ayyūb's name – the name upon which this chain of narrators turns – which caused all these other men, including Ḥammād,

Sufyān, ʿAbd al-Wārith and others, to be willing to relate the hadith on his authority, with the result that it gained wide circulation and acceptance despite its questionable content.

(2) *Ḥammād ibn Zayd*: Al-Bukhārī (6922): "...some unbelievers were brought to ʿAlī, who cast them into a fire. News of this reached Ibn ʿAbbās, who said, 'If I had been in his place, I would not have cast them into a fire, since the Messenger of God forbade us to do such things, saying, "Do not inflict on others a chastisement like that which God will inflict [on human beings in the afterlife]." Rather, I would have killed them based on the words of the Messenger of God, "If anyone changes his religion, put him to death."'"[16]

This hadith and/or the story is also mentioned by Aḥmad (1:282)[17], Abū Yaʿlā (2532)[18], Ibn Ḥabbān (5606)[19], al-Dārquṭnī (3:113)[20], and Ibn ʿAbd al-Barr who relates the hadith in *al-Tamhīd* (5:304)[21]. Al-Bayhaqī (8:202)[22] quote the same story.

(3) *Sufyān ibn ʿUyaynah*: Al-Bukhārī (3017) quotes the same story and hadith.[23] However, there is *tadlīs* in this chain of narrators.[24] Ibn Abī ʿUmar mentions this chain in his *Musnad*, as does Muḥammad ibn ʿAbbād on the authority of al-Ismāʿīlī, all of whom narrate the hadith on the authority of Sufyān, who states, "I saw ʿAmrū ibn Dīnār, Ayyūb and ʿAmmār al-Duhnī gathered together and recalling to each other those who had been burned by ʿAlī. Ayyūb said,...", whereupon he mentions the hadith. ʿAmmār said, "But he did not burn them. Rather, he dug trenches for them that opened onto each other, after which he [lit a fire and] exposed them to its smoke." However, ʿAmru ibn Dīnār quotes a poet as saying:

> Let death cast me wherever it wills
> If it casts me not into the two trenches!
> When they set the wood ablaze
> Death comes without delay.

Al-Ḥāfiẓ ibn Ḥajar states in *al-Fatḥ* (6:151):

> It seems that ʿAmru ibn Dīnār wishes in this manner to refute what was said by ʿAmmār al-Duhnī when he denied that the burning had taken place. Then, in the third part of the hadith passed down on the authority of Abū Ṭāhir al-Mukhallis I found [the words], "We were informed by Luwayn on the authority of Sufyān ibn ʿUyaynah," who cites the hadith on the authority of Ayyūb alone, then on the authority of ʿAmmār alone. Ibn ʿUyaynah states, "I mentioned it[25] to ʿAmru ibn Dīnār, and he denied it, saying, 'So what is the significance of the poet's words, "I lit my fire and called out to Qunbur"?'"

Al-Ḥāfiẓ then adds, "What I suspected thus appears to have been correct"! But what is it, exactly, that confirmed what al-Ḥāfiẓ had thought to be true? And what is it that he had thought to be true? Moreover, are events this significant confirmed in this manner?

Ibn ʿAbd al-Barr states in *al-Tamhīd* (5:316) that, "When Ibn ʿAbbās learned that ʿAlī had burned the apostates – that is, the unbelievers – he said, 'If I had been in his place, I would have killed them in keeping with the words of the Prophet, "If anyone changes his religion, put him to death." I would not have burned them with fire, since the Messenger of God said that no one is permitted to inflict on another the chastisement which God alone will inflict [in the afterlife].'"[26]

Sufyān said, "ʿAmmār al-Duhnī (who was seated in a gathering together with ʿAmru ibn Dīnār as Ayyūb was relating this hadith) said that ʿAlī had not burned them with fire, but, rather, had dug holes from which he exposed them to smoke until they died."

ʿAmru ibn Dīnār said, "But have you not heard the verse that says, 'May death cast me...?'", then quoted the two lines of poetry cited above.

The hadith is also related by Ibn Mājah (2535),[27] Ibn Abī Shaybah (9041),[28] Abū Yaʿlā (2532),[29] Al-Shāfiʿī (*Badāʾiʿ al-Minan*, 2:188–189),[30] who relates both the story and the hadith from the chain of narrators which includes al-Shāfiʿī, al-Bayhaqī (8:195),[31] and Al-Baghawī (*Sharḥ al-Sunnah*, 2561) who likewise cites the chain of narrators which includes al-Shāfiʿī.[32]

(4) *ʿAbd al-Wārith ibn Saʿīd, Wuhayb ibn Khālid*: Al-Nasā'ī (7:104) relates the same story and the hadith in two versions.[33, 34]

(5) *Maʿmar ibn Rāshid*: ʿAbd al-Razzāq quotes the hadith in his *Muṣannaf* (18706), "We were informed by Maʿmar, on the authority of Ayyūb, on the authority of ʿIkrimah, on the authority of Ibn ʿAbbās, that 'The Messenger of God said, "If anyone changes (or turns back from) his religion, put him to death, but do not inflict on others the chastisement with which God will chastise [human beings in the afterlife],"'" that is, fire. Al-Nasā'ī (7:104) cites the same hadith[35], and so does Ibn Ḥabbān (4476).

There is a biographical entry on ʿAlī ibn Ziyād al-Laḥjī in *al-Thiqāt* (8:470) according to which, "He [ʿAlī ibn Ziyād al-Laḥji] is reliable in the hadiths he transmits." As for Abū Qurrah, he is Mūsā ibn Ṭāriq al-Yamānī, who has also been declared reliable.

Al-Ḥāfiẓ Tammām al-Rāzī states in his *Fawā'id* (*Zawā'id al-Ajzā' al-Manthūrah*, 440), "I was informed by Abū al-Ḥasan ʿAlī ibn al-Ḥasan ibn ʿAllān al-Ḥāfiẓ on the authority of al-Mufaḍḍal ibn Muḥammad al-Jundī," who relates the hadith with the chain of transmission given by Ibn Ḥabbān and with the text mentioned earlier. Moreover, at the end of the hadith he adds, "And the Messenger of God prohibited the mutilation of corpses."

(6) *Saʿīd ibn Iyyās al-Jarīri, Saʿīd ibn Abī ʿUrūbah*: In *Sharḥ al-Sunnah* (2560), al-Baghawī states the hadith.[36] Al-Dārquṭnī mentions the hadith with two different chains(3:113).[37, 38]

(7) *ʿAbd al-Wahhāb ibn ʿAbd al-Majīd al-Thaqafī*: Al-Tirmidhī (1458) writes that ʿAlī burned by fire some people who had apostatized from Islam. When news of this reached Ibn ʿAbbās, he said, "If I had been in his place, I would have killed them in keeping with the saying of the Prophet, 'If anyone changes his religion, put him to death.' I would not have burned them, since the Messenger of God said, 'Do not inflict on others a chastisement like that which God will inflict [on human beings in the afterlife].'" And when news of what Ibn ʿAbbās had said reached ʿAlī, he said, "Ibn ʿAbbās is

right."[39] Abū Īsā al-Tirmidhī states, "This is a sound, good hadith, and scholars have relied on it in relation to the matter of how to deal with the apostate."

(8) *Jarīr ibn Ḥāzim*: The hadith is narrated with the aforementioned chain of transmission by al-Bayhaqī (8:202), who traces it back to Yaʿqūb ibn Sufyān and Ismāʿīl al-Qāḍī (Hadith A-6), who said, "We were informed by Sulaymān ibn Ḥarb on the authority of Jarīr ibn Ḥāzim on the authority of Ayyūb...", after which both the story and the hadith are mentioned. In addition, al-Bayhaqī adds the words, "When news of what Ibn ʿAbbās had said reached ʿAlī, he said, 'Woe to Ibn Umm al-Faḍl (that is, Ibn ʿAbbās)! He is keen to point out [other people's] mistakes.'"

(9) *Ismāʿīl ibn Ibrāhīm ibn ʿUlayyah*: Abū Dāwūd states in his *Sunan* (*ʿAwn al-Maʿbūd*, 3:12) mentions both the story and the hadith.[40] The end of the hadith reads, "When news of what Ibn ʿAbbās had said reached ʿAlī, he said, 'Woe to Ibn ʿAbbās!'" In *al-Tamhīd* (5:305), Ibn ʿAbd al-Barr cites the chain of narrators that includes Abū Dāwūd.[41]

This hadith has also been narrated in other versions on the authority of Ibn ʿUlayyah on the authority of Maʿmar, on the authority of Ayyūb.[42] However, there are some who have not recognized them. It is an established fact that Ibn ʿUlayyah heard accounts from Maʿmar and Ayyūb; however, some have said, "It often happens that a disciple will hear an account from his shaykh indirectly (through someone else), after which he hears it from his shaykh directly." As for Qatādah's and al-Ḥakam's account which agrees with ʿIkrimah's, it has been narrated as below.

(10) *Qatādah's* parallel account: Al-Nasā'ī (7:104) mentions this hadith with Qatādah in the chain of narrators.[43] Al-Nasā'ī (7:104–105) also mentions the hadith with a chain of transmission that only goes back to the second generation after the Prophet.[44]

Al-Nasā'ī then comments, saying, "This is more likely to be sound than the hadith passed down through ʿAbbād. The reason for this is that, although ʿAbbād has been declared by hadith scholars to be a trustworthy narrator, there is confusion and inconsistency in the hadith he narrates on the authority of Saʿīd ibn Abī ʿUrūbah; this is also what Imam Aḥmad has to say concerning what al-Athram narrated on his authority.

As for Muḥammad ibn Bishr, he is al-ʿAbdī Abū ʿAbd Allāh al-Kūfī, and according to what al-Ḥāfiẓ has to say about him in *al-Taqrīb*, he was a reliable narrator who had memorized the Qur'an in its entirety. When al-Ājurrī asked Abū Dāwūd about Muḥammad ibn Bishr's having heard reports from Saʿīd ibn Abī ʿUrūbah, he replied, 'He had memorized more [hadiths] than anyone else in all of Kufa.'

This being the case, Muḥammad ibn Bishr's account related on the authority of Saʿīd is to be preferred over that narrated by ʿAbbād ibn al-ʿAwwām, particularly if ʿAbbād ibn al-ʿAwwām's account differs with that of other narrators." It might be added here that this hadith has been documented on the authority of Qatādah in other versions as passed down on the authority of Anas, on the authority of Ibn ʿAbbās.

(11) *Al-Ḥakam ibn Abān's* parallel version: This version is related in *al-Kabīr* (11617) by al-Ṭabarānī. It states that the Messenger of God said, "If anyone's religion conflicts with that of the Muslims, cut off his head. However, if such a person bears witness that there is no god but God and that Muhammad is His Messenger, no punishment may be inflicted upon him unless he commits some crime deserving thereof."[45]

This hadith has a weak chain of transmission owing to the weakness of Ibrāhīm ibn al-Ḥakam ibn Abān as a narrator. In al-Dūrī's account as passed down on the authority of Yaḥyā ibn Maʿīn, he states, "None of the hadiths in his books (that is, those narrated by Ibrāhīm ibn al-Ḥakam ibn Abān's father on the authority of ʿIkrimah) has a chain of transmission that goes further back than the second generation after the Prophet, nor does it contain the names of Ibn ʿAbbās or Abū Hurayrah."

Ibn ʿUdayy states, "The distressing thing is the report according to which he claimed that the hadiths he narrated on the authority of his father – which were all *mursal* – were attributable to the Prophet himself. Most of the hadiths he narrated lacked parallel accounts from other narrators. And on top of this, we have the distressing content of the hadith itself."

Next, we consider the chain of narrators that contains Qatādah's name and which rests on the authority of Anas and Ibn ʿAbbās

(12) *Qatādah's* account: Hishām ibn Abī ʿAbd Allāh al-Dastawā'ī: This account is related by al-Nasā'ī (7:105)[46], al-Nasā'ī,[47] Aḥmad (1:322–323),[48] Abū Yaʿlā (2533),[49] Ibn Ḥabbān (4475),[50] Al-Ṭabarānī,[51] and al-Bayhaqī (8:202).[52]

Along with what has already been mentioned in relation to the story of the Caliph ʿAlī ibn Abī Ṭālib's burning a group of unbelievers or apostates with fire, one may add the other chains of narrators through which the account has been passed down to us. For despite the flaws in these chains, hadith scholars have not hesitated to narrate and repeat this story time after time, attempting to establish its reliability.

Ibn Abī Shaybah (9052) relates[53], that "people were worshipping idols in secret while benefiting from money given to them out of the Muslim state treasury. ʿAlī brought them in and put them in prison, then consulted with the people as to what he should do with them. 'Kill them,' the people said. 'No,' he replied. 'Instead, I will do to them what was done to our father Abraham,' whereupon he burned them with fire"!!

My own response to this is to say: This is a veritable disaster, as it calls into question the soundness of the faith of the people of that era overall.

Ibn Abī Shaybah (9053) also writes, "We were informed by Marwān ibn Muʿāwiyah, on the authority of Ayyūb ibn al-Nuʿmān, who said, 'I saw ʿAlī in the public square. A man approached him and said, "The inhabitants of one of the houses here have an idol inside, and they are worshipping it." ʿAlī rose and went to the house, and they brought a marble statue out to him. Then he burned the house down on top of them.'"

In the third part of his hadith, Abū Ṭāhir al-Mukhalliṣ relates[54], that ʿAlī was told that there were people at the mosque door claiming that he was their Lord. ʿAlī summoned them and said to them, "Woe be to you. What are you saying?" "You are our Lord, our Creator and our Sustainer," they replied. "Woe to you!" he repeated. "I am nothing but a human being like you. I eat food just as you do, and I drink just as you do. When I obey God, He rewards me if He so wills, and if I disobey Him, I fear His chastisement. So, fear God, and turn back [from this claim of yours]!" However, they refused to do so. They came back to see him the following morning, and Qunbur came and said, "I tell you truly, they have gone back to saying the same things." "Bring them in," ʿAlī instructed him. But they said the same things they had been saying before.

On the third day, [ʿAlī] said, "If you utter these words one more time, I will most surely put you to death in the most terrible way." However, they insisted on speaking in the same manner. "Qunbur," he said, "bring me some workers with picks and shovels. Then dig a trench for them that extends from the door of the mosque to the palace." Then he added, "Dig the trench deep." He brought the firewood and cast it into the fire in the trench, saying, "I will throw you into this fire unless you recant the things you have been saying." But they refused, so he cast them into it until they were burned, saying:

> When I set my eyes on something abominable, I set my fire ablaze and call for Qunbur.

In *al-Fatḥ* (12:270), al-Ḥāfiẓ states, "This has a good chain of transmission." Ibn ʿAbd al-Barr states in *al-Tamhīd* (5:317), "We have related, in various versions, the account according to which ʿAlī only burned these people after putting them to death." He then provides a chain of transmission via Khārijah ibn Muṣʿab on the authority of Sallām ibn Abī al-Qāsim, on the authority of ʿUthmān ibn Abī ʿUthmān al-Anṣārī, who said, "Some Shiites came to ʿAlī and declared, 'O Commander of the Faithful, you are He.' 'Who am I?'

he asked. 'You are He,' they replied, 'Woe be to you! Who am I?' he said. 'You are our Lord.' 'Woe be to you! Take back what you just said and repent.' However, they refused, so he beheaded them. Then he said, 'Qunbur, bring me bundles of firewood.' He then dug a trench for them in the ground and burned them in the fire, after which he recited the verse, 'When I set my eyes....'," and the rest of the line of poetry. Those who deified Imam ʿAlī and to whom he set fire are thus described as Shiites!

The hadith has also been cited as it has been related based on the account of Muʿāwiyah ibn Ḥaydah, al-Ṭabarānī states in *al-Kabīr* (19:419)[55], that the Messenger of God said, "If anyone changes his religion, put him to death. God will not accept the repentance of someone who has reverted to unbelief after entering Islam."[56]

The response is: If this hadith is sound, why all the debate over the matter of giving an apostate an opportunity to repent?

This hadith has also been related on the authority of ʿĀ'ishah, righteous mother of the faithful. Al-Ṭabarānī states in *al-Awsaṭ* (9226) that "The Messenger of God said, 'If anyone changes his religion, put him to death.'"[57] Al-Ṭabarānī states, "This hadith is only narrated on ʿĀ'ishah's authority with this chain of transmission, which is provided by none but Mūsā ibn Ayyūb." Al-Haythamī (6:261) states, "It [this chain of transmission] includes Abū Bakr al-Hudhalī, who is a weak narrator," after which he cites the hadith.

(13) *Abū Hurayrah's*: Al-Ṭabarānī quotes this hadith in *al-Awsaṭ* (8618) and adds, "The only person who relates this hadith on the authority of Bukayr is Ibn Lahīʿah."[58] As for al-Haythamī, he declares its chain of transmission to be good.

There is a well-known dispute over the reliability of Ibn Lahīʿah. Nevertheless, al-Haythamī declares the hadith to be a good one based on this chain of transmission despite the fact that the majority of hadith scholars have declared it to be weak. And if Ibn Lahīʿah is considered a weak narrator, what are we to say of a hadith which he is the only one to have transmitted?

In a biographical sketch of Isḥāq ibn ʿAbd Allāh ibn Abī Farwah which appears in *al-Kāmil* (1:322), Ibn ʿUdayy states that the

Prophet declared, "If anyone changes his religion, behead him."[59] Ibn ʿUdayy states, "With regard to the reports I have mentioned here from this Isḥāq ibn Abī Farwah and the chains of transmission he provides, [it bears noting that] no one agrees with his chains of transmission, nor with the content of his narratives. Moreover, his other reports which I have not mentioned here resemble the ones I have mentioned. Hence, he is clearly a weak narrator." Despite this fact, al-Layth ibn Saʿd relates a long account on his authority. Be that as it may, the most important information to be gleaned from the account is that the incident described took place in Madinah.

(14) *ʿIṣmah's*: Al-Ṭabarānī (17:186) mentions a long version of the hadith with a chain of transmission, part of which is on the authority of ʿIṣmah and includes al-Faḍl ibn al-Mukhtār.[60] Al-Haythamī states in *al-Majmaʿ* (6:261), "This [chain of transmission] includes al-Faḍl ibn al-Mukhtār, who is a weak narrator."

(15) *Ibn ʿUmar*: Ibn ʿAbd al-Barr quotes the hadith in *al-Tamhīd* (5:304) with ibn ʿUmar in the chain.[61] Ibn ʿAbd al-Barr writes, "This hadith is to be rejected (*munkar*). And God knows best." His statement in full will be quoted in the discussion below of the incompletely transmitted hadith associated with Zayd ibn Aslam.

Yet, in spite of this, and as seen earlier, Ibn ʿAbd al-Barr states categorically that there is no disagreement among Muslims concerning the validity of the death penalty for the apostate, and that there has been no inconsistency among the Prophetic hadiths and the Sunnah on this matter!

(16) *Al-Ḥasan al-Baṣrī* (incompletely transmitted): Al-Nasā'ī (7:104–105) cites the hadith with an incomplete transmission.[62]

What al-Nasā'ī has to say about this in his discussion of the hadith passed down on the authority of Saʿīd ibn Abī ʿUrūbah has already been stated. It is also related by al-Ḥārith ibn Abī Usāmah in his *Musnad* (page 132 of his appendices) based on what al-Albani states in *Irwā' al-Ghalīl* (8:125).

(17) *Zayd ibn Aslam* (incompletely transmitted): Mālik states in *al-Muwaṭṭa'* (2:211) with al-Suyūṭī's commentary, "[It has been narrated] on the authority of Zayd ibn Aslam that the Messenger of God said, 'If anyone changes his religion, behead him.'" Ibn ʿAbd al-Barr states in *al-Tamhīd* (5:304):

> Thus, the group of narrators cited in *al-Muwaṭṭa'* relate it with an incomplete chain of transmission. Nothing sound concerning this matter has been transmitted by Mālik with the exception of this incompletely transmitted hadith on the authority of Zayd ibn Islam. It has been related on the authority of Mālik, on the authority of Nāfiʿ, on the authority of Ibn ʿUmar that the Prophet said, "If anyone changes his religion, put him to death." However, this hadith is to be rejected (*munkar*) in my view. And God knows best.

TEXTUAL EVIDENCE SUPPORTING THE HADITH

This hadith has textual evidence in support of it on the authority of Muʿādh ibn Jabal, ʿAlī ibn Abī Ṭālib, ʿAbd Allāh ibn Masʿūd, and ʿUthmān ibn ʿAffān.

(1) *Muʿādh:* Al-Ṭabarānī states in *al-Kabīr* (20:53–54) and in *Musnad al-Shāmiyīn* (3576), that the Messenger of God told Muʿādh ibn Jabal when he sent him to Yemen, 'Any man who turns away from Islam, invite him [to return], and if he repents, accept his repentance. If he does not repent, however, behead him. Similarly, if any woman turns away from Islam, invite her [to return], and if she returns, accept this from her. And if she refuses, [continued to] urge her to repent.'[63]

Al-Haythamī (6:263) states, "[This chain of transmission] includes an unnamed narrator. Makḥūl states [that the unknown narrator is] Ibn Abī Ṭalḥah al-Yaʿmurī. As for the other narrators, they are trustworthy."

Al-Ḥāfiẓ ibn Ḥajar al-ʿAsqalānī states in *al-Fatḥ* (12:272), "Its chain of transmission is sound. [Moreover, this hadith] speaks explicitly concerning the issue in dispute (that is, concerning the matter of putting the female apostate to death); hence, it must be treated as an authoritative point of reference." How amazing! As long as it reinforces his juridical point of view concerning apostates, he stipulates the necessity of treating it as an authoritative point of reference without regard for the problems relating to its chain of transmission, including an unknown narrator and its inconsistency with the explicit content of the Qur'an and the action-based Sunnah of the Prophet!

In fact, one can go further than this and say: Its chain of transmission is weak. Al-Fazārī is Muḥammad ibn ʿUbayd Allāh al-ʿAzramī, and he is not to be relied upon. Consequently, one fails to see on what basis al-Haythamī declares the remaining narrators in this chain of transmission to be reliable, or on what basis al-Ḥāfiẓ declares its chain of transmission to be good, unless these two scholars have taken al-Fazārī to be Abū Isḥāq al-Fazārī, that is, Ibrāhīm ibn Muḥammad ibn al-Ḥārith, who had memorized the Qur'an in its entirety, who was a trustworthy narrator, and on whose authority Muḥammad ibn Salamah, that is, al-Ḥarrānī, narrates a version of the hadith in Ibn Mājah. However, Abū Isḥāq [al-Fazārī] relates no account on the authority of Makḥūl. Rather, the narrator who has passed down accounts on Makḥūl's authority, and on whose authority Muḥammad ibn Salamah has passed down accounts is al-ʿAzramī, who, as we have seen, is unreliable. Ibn ʿUdayy has drawn attention to the fact that it is he [al-ʿAzramī] who is meant by most of what Muḥammad ibn Salamah narrates; however, when he says 'al-Fazārī', he identifies only his place of his origin [Fazār], yet without identifying him more specifically.

As for Ibn Abī Ṭalḥah, he is Maʿdān, a reliable narrator whose hadiths have been related by Muslim and the four.[64] However, Makḥūl does not demonstrate that the narrator who was not named is Maʿdān, nor does he mention anything to support his supposition.

(2) *Abū Bakr* the Righteous: The traditions which have been narrated concerning Abū Bakr from the time of the 'wars of apostasy' are general in nature and quite numerous. They may be referred to in their original sources,[65] which include: a) What is narrated by Abū Yaʿlā in *al-Maṭālib al-ʿĀliyah* (2:113–114) and by Ibn ʿAbd

al-Barr in *al-Tamhīd* (5:314) concerning the apostasy of the tribe of Banū ʿĀmir in particular. Both of these scholars quote al-Shaʿbī, who said, "The tribe of Banū ʿĀmir apostatized and murdered the workers among them who had been sent out by the Messenger of God, then set fire to them. Abū Bakr wrote to Khālid with orders to kill Banū ʿĀmir and to burn them with fire."

Here also we need to pause briefly to inquire about Banū ʿĀmir: Were they a large tribe or a small one? How many individuals belonged to their community? Did all of them take part in this despicable crime, or just some of them? Did the burning of Banū ʿĀmir actually take place? And which of the Companions witnessed it, particularly among Khālid's soldiers, who are supposed to have carried it out?

b) What is narrated by Ibn ʿAbd al-Barr in *al-Tamhīd* (5:314–315), where he writes, "When al-Fujā'ah – namely, Iyyās ibn ʿAbd Allāh ibn ʿAbd Yālīl – apostatized, Abū Bakr sent al-Zubayr ibn al-ʿAwāmm out to him with thirty men on horseback. Al-Zubayr ibn al-ʿAwāmm waited until nightfall, then took al-Fujā'ah. He then returned to Abū Bakr, who said, 'Take him out to the place of prayer and burn him with fire,' and his orders were carried out."

(3) *ʿAlī ibn Abī Ṭālib*: Among the things which have been narrated concerning ʿAlī ibn Abī Ṭālib in this connection is what is mentioned by Ibn Abī Shaybah (9035), who writes, "The apostate is to be given three opportunities to repent. If he repents, [his repentance is to be accepted], but if he does not, he is to be killed." Al-Bayhaqī (8:207) also narrates this account based on the chain of narrators that includes Ibn Abī Shaybah.

ʿAbd al-Razzāq narrates on the authority of Abū ʿUthmān al-Nahdī that ʿAlī urged a man who had reverted to unbelief after entering Islam to repent, but he refused, so he killed him.

It is related on the authority of Abū ʿAmr al-Shaybānī that a man of the tribe of Banū ʿIjl became a Christian, whereupon ʿUyaynah ibn Farqad al-Sulamī wrote concerning this to ʿAlī ibn Abī Ṭālib. ʿAlī wrote back with instructions for the man to be brought in. A long-haired man clad in rough woolen clothing, Abū ʿAmr al-Shaybānī was brought in bound in shackles. ʿAlī spoke to him at length but he remained silent the entire time. Then he said, "I do not know what you are saying. All I know is that Jesus is the Son of God." When the man said this, ʿAlī rose and trampled him underfoot. When the people saw that ʿAlī had trampled the man underfoot, they rose and did the same, after which ʿAlī gave instructions for the man to be burned with fire.

According to another version of the same account, ʿAlī said to the man, "It may be that you have only apostatized in order to collect an inheritance, after which you intend to return to Islam." Then he continued, saying, "Perhaps you wanted to marry a [Christian] girl and her family refused to give her to you, so you decided to convert to Christianity until you were married, after which you were intending to embrace Islam again." "That is not the case," the man replied. "So return to Islam," said ʿAlī. "No," said the man, "not until I meet Christ." ʿAlī then gave instructions for the man to be beheaded, and he was killed, and his inheritance was given to his Muslim children.

Another version relates that al-Miswar al-ʿIjlī became a Christian after having embraced Islam. ʿUtbah ibn Abī Waqqāṣ then sent him to ʿAlī, who urged him to repent. However, he refused, and ʿAlī killed him. The Christians requested his body in return for 30,000 [dirhams] but ʿAlī refused to give it to them, after which he burned it.

ʿUbādah narrates on the authority of al-ʿAlā' Abū Muḥammad that ʿAlī took a man from the tribe of Bakr ibn Wā'il who had become a Christian after having embraced Islam. He proposed that the man return to Islam over a period of a month, but he refused, so he killed him. This account is mentioned by Ibn Ḥazm in *al-Muḥallā* (13:123), and by Ibn ʿAbd al-Barr in *al-Tamhīd* (5:308–309) without a chain of transmission. A similar account is narrated by Ibn Abī Shaybah (9056) and ʿAbd al-Razzāq (10:170), while an abbreviated version of the same is narrated by Saʿīd ibn Manṣūr in his *Sunan*.

In *al-Awsaṭ*, al-Ṭabarānī relates on the authority of Suwayd ibn Ghaflah that ʿAlī was told that a group of people had apostatized from Islam. ʿAlī sent to them and fed them, then invited them to return to Islam, but they refused. ʿAlī then dug a hole, brought them in and beheaded them. He cast their bodies into the hole, threw firewood on top of them and set fire to them, saying, "Truly have God and His Messenger spoken." Al-Ḥāfiẓ mentions this account in *al-Fatḥ* (12:270) without comment. Amazingly, it has been said that his silence concerning the account means that he judged it to be trustworthy, in keeping with al-Ḥāfiẓ's usual approach.

Ibn Abī Shaybah (9051) relates[66] that ʿAlī burned some unbelievers in the market, and that when he threw the fire on them he said, "Truly have God and His Messenger spoken." Then he departed. [Suwayd states,] "So I followed him and he said, 'Is that you, Suwayd?' 'Yes, O Commander of the Faithful. I heard you saying something.' 'Suwayd,' he replied, 'I am with ignorant people, so if you hear me say, "Thus said the Messenger of God," it is the truth.'"

Both of these two traditions are astounding in every respect. First of all, there is a single narrator, namely, Suwayd ibn Ghaflah. Hence, in the tradition as it is related by al-Ṭabarānī, we find that Imam ʿAlī sent for the apostates and fed them, he invited them to return to Islam, they refused, and so forth. However, there is no indication of who these people were, what their apostasy consisted in, how many there were of them, when it took place, or who witnessed these events. As for the same tradition as related by Ibn Abī Shaybah, it specifies that Imam ʿAlī did what he did in the marketplace. What this means is that the people present in the marketplace at the time witnessed what happened. So how is it possible that no one but Suwayd related the event, or that no one but he followed the Imam out of the marketplace as he left following this harrowing incident in order to ask what the Imam meant by his statement, "Truly have God and His Messenger spoken"?!

His statement in the account passed down by Ibn Abī Shaybah, "I am with ignorant people, so if you hear me say, 'Thus said the Messenger of God,' it is the truth" appears in another tradition which has been narrated on his authority as well. In this other tradition ʿAlī is quoted as saying, "I am simply a warrior who speaks in times of contentment and discontent. However, if I say, 'Thus said the Messenger of God,' I will never speak an untruth concerning him." Given that each of the two accounts deals with a separate incident, might they have been combined or confused?

Be that as it may, these traditions passed down concerning ʿAlī may bear a close connection to the events relating to the verse we examined earlier in *Sūrah Āl ʿImrān.*

(4) *ʿUthmān ibn ʿAffān*: ʿAbd al-Razzāq narrates concerning ʿUthmān ibn ʿAffān (with a chain of narrators that includes Ibn Ḥazm in *al-Muḥallā* [13:123]) according to which someone apostatized from Islam after coming to believe. ʿUthmān invited the man three times to return to Islam, the man refused, and ʿUthmān killed him.

ʿAbd al-Razzāq (10:168) narrates on the authority of ʿAbd Allāh ibn ʿUtbah ibn Masʿūd that he (Ibn Masʿūd) captured some natives of Iraq who had apostatized from Islam. He then wrote concerning them to ʿUthmān. ʿUthmān wrote back in reply that he should propose that they accept the religion of truth and bear witness that there is no god but God. If they agreed, Ibn Masʿūd was to let them go their way, and if they refused, he was to kill them. Some of them agreed to re-enter Islam, and he let them go, while others refused, and he killed them.

(5) *Other narrators*: It is narrated concerning ʿAbd Allāh ibn ʿUmar that he said, "The apostate is to be given three opportunities to repent and return to Islam. If he repents, he is to be left alone, and if he refuses, he is to be killed." This tradition is related by Ibn Abī Shaybah (9036) with a chain of narrators that includes al-Bayhaqī (8:207).

Mūsā ibn ʿUqbah relates on the authority of Ibn Shihāb concerning the apostasy of [the tribes of] Asad and Ghaṭafān during the Battle of Buzākhah that "they fought fiercely [against the Muslims], and the Muslims felled a large number of their enemies while taking others captive. Khālid then gave instructions for an enclosure to be built, after which he lit a huge fire beneath it and cast the captives into it." This tradition is mentioned by Ibn ʿAbd al-Barr in *al-Tamhīd* (5:315–316).

It is related that when ʿUbayd ibn ʿUmayr was asked about a man who commits apostasy after becoming a Muslim, he said, "He is to be killed." The tradition is narrated by Ibn Abī Shaybah (9040).

It is related that ʿUmar ibn ʿAbd al-ʿAziz said, "The apostate should be given three days to repent. If he returns to Islam during this time [he will be left alone] and if he refuses, he is to be killed." This tradition is related by Ibn Saʿd in ʿUmar's biographical sketch in *al-Ṭabaqāt al-Kubrā*, and it is attributed to him by al-Zaylaʿī in *Naṣb al-Rāyah* (3:461).

It is related that ʿAṭā' ibn Abī Rabāḥ said that if someone apostatizes after entering Islam, he is to be invited to return to Islam, and if he refuses to do so, he is to be killed. This tradition is related by Ibn Abī Shaybah (9039) and ʿAbd al-Razzāq (10:164).

Al-Zuhrī is reported to have said, "[The apostate] is to be invited three times to return to Islam and if he refuses he is to be beheaded." This tradition is related by Ibn Abī Shaybah (9038) and ʿAbd al-Razzāq (10:164).

The aforementioned traditions appear in many traditional Islamic writings and compilations with slight variations in wording, and the reader may refer to them to verify this. In many of these traditions we find elements that raise questions. For example: Did Caliph ʿAlī's opponents want to alienate people from him by branding him as a cruel, tyrannical man? Given that the Messenger of God had informed ʿAlī that he would be his proxy in Madinah when he went out to battle, and that ʿAlī was to the Prophet as Aaron had been to Moses, did ʿAlī's opponents want to liken him, by way of suggestion, to the idolatrous people of Abraham?

In addition to noting the problems in these accounts' chains of transmission, it should be remembered that many of them are related by a single narrator. In addition, they are related in forms that call for further investigation because, if the events to which they refer really took place, people would have been shouting them from the housetops, as it were.

Some of the accounts that mention the act of burning apostates or unbelievers with fire make no mention of whether the burning took place after these people had been put to death by the sword, or whether they were burned alive. Additionally, we note that many of these accounts are marked by severe confusion and inconsistencies in relation to this point. Hence, we find that numerous questions can be raised about every one of these traditions relating to its chain of transmission, its content, and its implications. This being the case, this study has included a careful review of all these accounts together with their chains of narrators in order to help readers to see the difficulties they present us with. In short, such a study makes clear that an account's having been passed down via numerous chains of narrators guarantees neither the soundness of its content nor its validity.

This study has also sought to show the importance of allowing the Qur'an to reign supreme over the Sunnah. In other words, it is the Qur'an which verifies the truthfulness of the Sunnah, and not vice-versa. When this fact is clearly established, and when the Sunnah takes its natural place as that which revolves in the Qur'an's orbit, as it were, this will serve to prevent the kind of harm that results from the Sunnah's standing independently of the Qur'an or revolving in an orbit of its own.

When one ties the Sunnah securely to the Qur'an, one begins to perceive the mutual complementarity between them, which in turn makes it possible for us to overcome the problems that are raised in relation to hadith literature. Then, even when faced with weak or defective accounts, there is no longer any need to be preoccupied with debate over their chains of transmission, how they are to be understood, or how they apply to Islamic jurisprudence so long as there is a sound, authentic core which is consistent with the Qur'an.

5

MUSLIM JURISTS' VIEWS ON THE PENALTY FOR APOSTASY

PRELIMINARY REMARKS

At this point in this discussion the honorable, enlightened stance taken by the Qur'an on the matter of freedom of religion and the ways in which the Prophet's words and deeds serve to apply and clarify the Qur'anic teaching has come to the forefront. In addition, the study has brought to light the attitudes of the two rightly guided caliphs, Abū Bakr and ʿUmar ibn al-Khaṭṭāb, based on their commitment to the guidance brought by the Qur'an and the Sunnah. Given the foregoing, one comes to the question of what stance has been taken on this matter by Islamic jurisprudence and its jurists, and the evidence on which they have based this stance.

Muslim jurists base their positions on this issue on two foundations. The first of these is the verbal Sunnah, that is, words spoken by the Prophet. This foundation is based in turn on the view that the hadith, "If anyone changes his religion, put him to death" is sound. In addition, it rests on a generalized application of this hadith to everyone who changes his religion, whether or not he has waged war on Islam and Muslims. We have examined this hadith's content and its chain of transmission, and as we saw earlier, it is impossible to use it as a basis for juristic rulings unless it is seen in light of the malicious plot hatched by some followers of the Mosaic revelation – described in the passage quoted earlier from *Sūrah Āl ʿImran*[1] – to destroy the inward foundations of the Muslim community.

As for the second foundation, it is the claim to consensus. However, even with scholars' differing points of view concerning what constitutes a 'consensus', there can be no denying the fact that

Islam's schools of jurisprudence have differed widely amongst themselves on this point. Indeed, there have been such major differences of opinion within single schools that it would be very difficult to claim the existence of any kind of consensus.

Most of the recognized schools of jurisprudence have confused apostasy in the political sense with apostasy in the sense of a change in personal beliefs and convictions. Some schools have held that apostasy from Islam is a crime for which there is a divinely ordained punishment which must be enforced without any lenience whatsoever. Others have held that apostasy is a crime for which there is simply a discretionary punishment, while a third group has maintained that the punishment for apostasy falls within the realm of 'Islamic legal policies', and that Muslim rulers are free to apply it in accordance with their own interpretations thereof in order to preserve law, public order and the unity of the community. Some schools have distinguished between the varying circumstances that apply to apostates, thereby declaring some to be actual apostates, and not others. All of this confirms an undeniable fact, namely, that there is no consensus on this issue on the basis of which one might argue for the existence of a divinely prescribed punishment for apostasy. Moreover, even if we agreed, for the sake of argument, that such a consensus existed, it would be a consensus devoid of any basis.

HOW DID THE CONFUSION BETWEEN 'POLITICAL' APOSTASY AND 'RELIGIOUS' APOSTASY COME ABOUT?

The confusion that has attended the process of defining and categorizing the issue of apostasy on the juristic level may be attributable in large part to certain additions that were made to the oral culture that prevailed in the Hejazi environment. This oral culture, whose influence we noted in Chapter One of this study, viewed it as necessary to kill anyone who left Judaism.

The following are additional factors of note:

(1) The Islamic conquests served to bring many countries – all of which had their own systems, customs, cultures and laws – within the jurisdiction of the Muslim nation. Such laws included, for example, those related to the shifting of allegiances, rebellion against the political and legal order, and so forth. The Byzantines, the Persians and others all had well-established laws and regulations which generated customs and cultures in the conquered lands, and which in turn made their way into the Muslim environment and began interacting with it. These laws, regulations, customs and cultures thus came to color the Muslim juristic mindset, if even only in the realm of categorizing issues and legal questions that called for juristic rulings. It should also be noted in this connection that prior to Islam, the Roman-Christian system was applied in the Levant.

(2) The causes behind the 'wars of apostasy' which took place during the caliphate of Abū Bakr (11–13 AH/632–634 CE) were not precisely defined. For although they were based on the political dimension, the religious dimension was referred to in statements by Abū Bakr such as, "I will most surely wage war against anyone who separates ritual prayer from zakah!" Moreover, because Abū Bakr was relying on a conception of 'religion' in its comprehensive sense in which legislation, authority, public order and governance all play a part, and because all of these things are included under the rubric of Shariʿah, no clear division was laid down between doctrine and law. The objection raised by ʿUmar ibn al-Khaṭṭāb was based on his supposition that those who were refusing to pay the zakah were still uttering the words, "There is no god but God," even if they were only doing so for the sake of the protection this offered them. By what right, then, ʿUmar asked, were they to be fought against? However, Abū Bakr drew ʿUmar's attention to a more comprehensive perspective, one that does not allow for the sort of compartmentalization that the insubordinate communities were advocating in an attempt to deceive and mislead. For their aim was to strike at the Muslim nation as an entity, as a system, as a divine law and way of life, and to return to the system that had prevailed before the advent of Islam.

Hence, the so-called 'wars of apostasy' were not waged in order to force those who had changed their personal beliefs to return to the beliefs they had abandoned. Rather, their purpose was to oblige citizens who had abandoned their obligations and duties as members of the Islamic Ummah, or as citizens of a state, to live up to such obligations. These obligations, of course, derived their legitimate force from the religion, and from the patriotic duty the religion imposed on citizens in its capacity as the source of legality and legitimacy. A citizen is required to respect the legitimate authorities and not to engage in any action that would threaten his or her nation's sovereignty, unity or territorial integrity. Similarly, the Muslim citizen was not permitted to threaten the Muslim nation with fragmentation and reversion to a tribal system which, in the past, had been the equivalent of what is known in modern parlance as mini-states.

Given the foregoing, let us now examine the various juristic schools' stances on this matter.

The Ḥanafī School

Imam Abū Ḥanīfah and the adherents of his school did not classify apostasy among the crimes for which there are divinely prescribed punishments. Rather, they discussed it in their writings under the heading of *siyar*, that is, the theme of jihad and topics related thereto. Examples of this classification may be found in books such as al-Ṭaḥāwī's *al-Mukhtaṣar fī al-Fiqh*, al-Kāsānī's *Badā'iᶜ al-Ṣanā'iᶜ*, and others.

Jurists of the Ḥanafī school declare without exception that the female apostate is not to be put to death.[2] If a boy who has reached the age of discretion commits apostasy, he is not to be killed, but simply imprisoned.[3] At the same time, they hold that it is necessary to put the adult male apostate to death, although they produce no Qur'anic evidence for this position. Instead, they content themselves with citation of the aforementioned hadith, "If anyone changes his religion, put him to death." They support this hadith based on the consensus that existed among the Prophet's Companions concerning the necessity of waging war on apostates during the caliphate of Abū Bakr. As we have seen, however, the issue of apostasy in Abū Bakr's era was not one of changing one's personal creed; rather, it was an issue of rebelling against the order that had been ushered in by Islam and against the laws whose foundations had been laid in the Qur'an, foremost among which was the payment of zakah. In other words, it had to do with shattering the society, fragmenting the Ummah the Messenger of God had established by divine command, and returning to the pre-Islamic tribal system. These tribes were still willing to bear witness to God's oneness, perform the ritual prayers, and acknowledge the prophethood and mission of the Messenger of God. Hence, their 'apostasy' was an act of turning back from the obligation to uphold the unity of the Ummah and a rejection of the public order, particularly as it pertained to the payment of zakah. As such, the apostasy of which these tribes were guilty does not serve as valid evidence of a consensus among the Companions concerning the necessity of executing the individual apostate who has changed his religion without breaking with the community and turning against it.

The fact that Ḥanafī jurists have discussed the issue of apostasy within the framework of what is referred to as *siyar*, which has to do with matters of jihad, armed conflict and the various effects to which it leads, serves as further evidence of their tendency to view apostasy in political terms. Otherwise, they would not have included rulings on apostates as a chapter in their book on *siyar* following their discussion of the various rulings on the 'two abodes', namely, 'the abode of Islam' and 'the abode of war.'[4]

It is not valid to argue that although the apostate has done nothing but change his personal beliefs, there remains the possibility that he would demonstrate hostility toward the Muslim Ummah and take up arms against it. In so doing, we are treating a mere possibility as though it were an actual fact, whereas in Islamic jurisprudence, a mere possibility does not provide a sufficient cause for taking a life through a divinely prescribed punishment; on the contrary, there must be definitive proof.

The Mālikī School

According to the Mālikīs, apostasy is a matter which falls within the same category as violations such as *al-baghī** and *al-zinā*, or unlawful sexual intercourse.[5]

The Mālikīs do not hold that apostasy is a crime for which is there is a divinely ordained punishment. In *al-Muwaṭṭa'*, Imam Mālik makes mention of *al-irtidād* in his 'book of rulings', where he cites the incompletely transmitted hadith according to which the Messenger of God said, "If anyone changes his religion, behead him." Imam Mālik explains the hadith saying:

> The meaning of what the Prophet said is, in our view, that if those who have changed their religion from Islam to something else [covertly], such as the *zanādiqah*[6] and others like them, are defeated, they are to be killed and not given any opportunity to repent. The reason for this is that it is not possible to know whether their repentance is sincere, and whether or not they are declaring themselves to be Muslims while concealing unbelief in their hearts. Hence, I do not believe that such people should be given any opportunity to repent, nor should any claim to have repented be accepted from them. As for those who leave Islam for something else and declare this openly, they should be given the opportunity to repent; if they repent, their repentance is to be accepted, but if they do not repent, they are to be killed. That is to say, if a group of people have thus left Islam, they are to be invited to return and repent; if they do so, this is to be accepted of them, and if they refuse, they are to be killed. This does not refer, as we see it – though God knows best – to those who have left Judaism for Christianity or Christianity for Judaism, nor anyone belonging to any faith other than Islam who changes his religion. Hence, the hadith is speaking of those who leave Islam for something else and who make this known publicly, and God knows best.

In what he mentions here, Imam Mālik does not indicate that he is speaking of a divinely ordained punishment; rather, he is speaking of something similar to what is known as 'Islamic legal policy' which, in his view, a Muslim ruler should adopt toward *zanādiqah*.[7] For he adheres to the apparent meaning of the words, "If anyone changes his religion..." as though he were interpreting the phrase "changes his religion" to refer to a change which someone brings about in the substance of his religion by, for example, changing the number of obligatory ritual prayers from five to four or six, or by altering the pillars or doctrine of the religion. This is what was done by Musaylimah the Liar, Ṭulayḥah al-Asadī, Sajāḥ and other would-be prophets who exempted their followers from some of the required ritual prayers and the payment of zakah and allowed them some things that are forbidden in Islam. It is these who, in Imam Mālik's view, are to be put to death even if they claim outwardly not to have changed their religion.

Similarly, he holds that we are not required to give such people the opportunity to repent, nor should their repentance be accepted. Moreover, he makes no distinction between someone who has entered some other religion, and someone who has changed his religion into something other than what it was originally.

Ibn Rushd the grandfather, a Mālikī, explains the killing of the apostate as resulting from the absence of a religion on the basis of which the apostate may be recognized. In a discussion of the *jizyah*, that is, the poll tax levied by a Muslim state on its non-Muslim subjects, he states:

> As for those from whom the *jizyah* is not collected by agreement of all Muslim jurisprudents, they are the unbelievers of Quraysh and apostates. In the case of apostates, this is due to the fact that they belong to no religion on the basis of which they may be recognized; this is in keeping with the words of the Prophet, "If anyone changes his religion, put him to death."[8]

Such scholars have thus equated the theoretical possibility that someone who has changed his religion might wage war on the Muslim community, and the concrete act of waging such war. As we have seen, however, such an equation is unwarranted in Islamic jurisprudence.

In sum, then, the Mālikī position on this issue is that the apostate must be put to death, man or woman. They make no distinction between male and female in this regard. They hold that there is a possibility that the apostate will break with the Muslim community and take up arms against it. Therefore, if he is overpowered before waging war, it is agreed unanimously that the man should be killed, whereas there is disagreement as to whether a woman apostate is to be killed straightaway, or whether she should first be given an opportunity to repent. The majority view among the Mālikīs is that the woman should be killed based on the most general application of the hadith, "If anyone changes his religion, put him to death." If, on the other hand, an apostate actually takes up arms against the Muslims and they then gain victory over him, he is to be killed based on the charge of having waged war on the Muslim community and is not to be given any opportunity to repent, and this whether the aggression took place on Muslim territory, or after the person had escaped to non-Muslim territory. The only exception to this is a situation in which the person converts back to Islam [of his own accord].[9]

The Shāfiʿī School[10]

Imam al-Shāfiʿī approached the issue of apostasy in light of the four following Qur'anic verses: (1) "And fight against them until there is no more oppression and all worship is devoted to God alone" (8:39); (2) "...slay those who ascribe divinity to aught beside God wherever you may come upon them, and take them captive, and besiege them, and lie in wait for them at every conceivable place. Yet if they repent, and take to prayer, and render the purifying dues,[11] let them go their way; for, behold, God is Much-Forgiving, a Dispenser of grace" (9:5); (3) "But if any of you should turn away from his faith and die as a denier of the truth – these it is whose works will go for nought in this world and in the life to come; and these it is who are destined for the fire, therein to abide" (2:217); and (4) "And yet, it has already been revealed to thee [O man,] as well as to those who lived before thee, that if thou ever ascribe divine powers to aught but God, all thy works shall most certainly have been in vain: for [in the life to come] thou shalt most certainly be among the lost" (39:65). Imam al-Shāfiʿī states:

We were informed by the trustworthy narrator, on the authority of Ḥammād ibn Zayd, on the authority of Yaḥyā ibn Saʿīd, on the authority of Abū Umāmah ibn Sahl, on the authority of ʿUthmān ibn ʿAffān, that the Messenger of God said, "No Muslim's life can lawfully be taken except in one of three cases: the reversion to unbelief after coming to faith, adultery, and murder."[12]

Al-Shāfiʿī then continues:

The statement of the Prophet, "No Muslim's life can lawfully be taken except in one of three cases," one of which is reversion to unbelief after faith, can only be taken to mean that 'unbelief' (*kufr*) is something which makes it lawful for the person who professes it to be put to death unless he repents.... God's ruling on killing the polytheists who did not become Muslims, His placing their possessions at the Muslims' disposal, in addition to the Prophet's ruling concerning reversion to unbelief after coming to faith appear to indicate – though God knows best – that if one's life is preserved through faith, after which it becomes lawful for one's life to be taken by virtue of one's leaving faith, then the ruling which applies to someone who has reverted to unbelief is the same as, if not more severe than, that which applies to someone who has been an unbeliever all along and is waging war on Muslims, since such a person has left the state [of belief] through which his life had been preserved and returned to the state [of unbelief] in which both his life and his property may be taken with impunity.

The apostate has committed a more serious crime than someone who has been a polytheist all along. The reason for this is that when someone reverts to ascribing divinity to entities other than God after having come to faith in God's oneness, God declares worthless all the good works this person had performed before this reversion. By contrast, if someone who was once ascribing divinity to beings other than God then surrenders to God in Islam, God will atone for all evil deeds the person may have committed before this. The Messenger of God made clear that if someone who had been a polytheist then

> became Muslim, all the sins he had committed prior to this would be atoned for. Speaking to a man who had done many righteous deeds during his days as a polytheist, the Prophet said, "Your Islam shall be added to the good you had already done." Moreover, it was the Prophet's custom, when he gained victory in battle over polytheists, to kill some of them, release some of them unconditionally, exchange some of them for Muslim captives taken by the enemy, and accept a ransom from some of them in return for their release. However, there was complete agreement among Muslims on the fact that it was not permissible for an apostate to be released in exchange for the release of a Muslim captive; nor was it permissible for an apostate to be released unconditionally, nor could a ransom be accepted from an apostate. Rather, the apostate had no choice but to return to Islam or be killed. And God knows best.[13]

By presenting the theme in this manner, and by relying on the four Qur'anic verses quoted above concerning the polytheists and the rulings which apply to them (*Sūrah al-Anfāl*: 39, *Sūrah al-Tawbah*: 5, *Sūrah al-Baqarah*: 217 and *Sūrah al-Zumar*: 65), al-Shāfiʿī attempts to draw an analogy between the apostate and a polytheist who must be put to death. In fact, he views the apostate as even more deserving of death than the polytheist. Similarly, he cites the hadith which combines reversion to unbelief after faith, adultery, and murder in order to argue based thereon that reversion to unbelief after faith renders it lawful to put someone to death. However, he does not state that the evidence upon which he has relied could be used to support the claim that there is a specific divinely ordained punishment in accordance with which the apostate must be put to death.

Now, returning to the details of al-Shāfiʿī's argument, one finds that the first verse he cites affirms the legitimacy of armed conflict as a means of protecting freedom of belief and warding off attempts to oblige people to change their religion by force, that is, through the use of torture and the like. The purpose for such armed conflict, moreover, was to win for those who lived on the Arabian Peninsula the freedom to abandon the age of ignorance and darkness and enter the religion of God – Islam – thereby fulfilling the words of God Almighty, "There shall be no compulsion is matters of faith." As for the act of breaking with the community and its associated law and order, this calls for specified penalties which fall under the category of divinely prescribed punishments, that is, "the bounds set by God," or appropriate discretionary punishments commensurate with the seriousness of the crime committed. As such, these punishments have nothing to do with changing one's creed.

As for the second verse cited by Imam al-Shāfiʿī, it deals with the pagan Arabs on whom God had commanded the Muslims to wage war in order for them to emerge from darkness into light, and from the ignorance of division, anarchy and lack of commitment to any system or order. In so doing, these people would become able to submit to an order, be transformed into part of a nation, and move beyond the type of ignorance that reduces human beings to a state lower than that of the animals. In so doing they would be purified and refined, come to merit respect, and become fit to perform the ritual prayers, pay zakah, and visit the Inviolable House of Worship (*al-bayt al-ḥarām*). These pagan Arabs were given four months in which to abandon their paganism and idol worship.

As for the final two verses, al-Shāfiʿī cites them in order to demonstrate that apostasy is more serious and more abhorrent than original unbelief based on the fact that apostasy results in one's works on earth losing all of their value, and the loss of the possibility of divine forgiveness. However, there is nothing in any of the four verses he cites that would indicate the necessity of a divinely ordained punishment for apostasy in the Qur'an. Hence, nothing he says or cites serves to negate the complete freedom that is affirmed by nearly two hundred verses in the Qur'an, all of which state, either explicitly or implicitly, that changing one's beliefs alone entails nothing but an accounting before God Almighty and His chastisement in the life to come.

As for the hadith Imam al-Shāfiʿī cites in an abbreviated form, it has been narrated by Muslim and others in a more extensive form, and with variant wordings. One of these variant versions appears in *Ṣaḥīḥ Muslim*, where we read that the Messenger of God said,

"There are only three cases in which the life of a Muslim who bears witness that there is no god but God and that I am God's Messenger may be lawfully taken, namely: adultery, murder, and abandonment of one's religion and the community [which represents it]." The version narrated by Aḥmad ibn Ḥanbal reads, "...abandonment of Islam and causing division in (or abandonment of) the community [which represents it]." What this means is that the life of a Muslim who belongs to the Islamic nation and who lives under an Islamic regime can only be lawfully taken under three conditions: (1) taking up sexual misconduct as a profession and promoting this practice among others in the society,[14] (2) premeditated murder, which calls for application of the law of retribution, and (3) abandonment of one's religion and turning against the community that represents it. This situation, however, is not our concern here, since what we are talking about is a divinely prescribed punishment for apostasy that consists in nothing more than an individual's changing his beliefs without breaking with the community of which he is a part or its legal system, without joining up with the enemies of the community to which this individual has belonged, and without abandoning or waging war on this community and the foundations upon which it rests. It is in light of this hadith that we must interpret all other hadiths with relevance to this same issue, including, for example, "If anyone changes his religion, put him to death." For when we do so its meaning becomes: If anyone changes his religion, abandons the community which represents it and sides with its enemies or takes up arms against it and attempts to sabotage its associated order, he must be put to death. The reason for this is that in such a case, the person is considered to have committed what is termed in modern parlance grand treason; such a person has sought to overturn the system upon which the community rests and its ruling regime, and plotted to harm the society.

Basing one's judgment on a concatenation of textual evidence and interpreting unqualified, that is, general, texts in light of qualified, or specific, ones, are acceptable and recognized practices in Islamic jurisprudence. For example, we interpret the verses which read, "[Thus speaks God]: 'O you servants of Mine who have transgressed against your own selves! Despair not of God's mercy; behold, God forgives all sins – for, verily, He alone is Much-Forgiving, a Dispenser of grace'" (39:53) and "Verily, God does not forgive the ascribing of divinity to aught beside Him, although He forgives any lesser sin unto whomever He wills: for he who ascribes divinity to aught beside God has indeed contrived an awesome sin" (4:48) in light of the verse which reads, "Yet withal, behold, I forgive all sins unto any who repents and attains to faith and does righteous deeds, and thereafter keeps to the right path" (20:82). For as noted earlier, it is an acceptable practice among Muslim scholars to interpret the unqualified in light of the qualified.

Imam al-Shāfiʿī concludes that the crime of which the apostate is guilty is more serious than that committed by someone who simply remains a polytheist. This conclusion is based on his supposition that the apostate will return to the polytheism which he had transcended previously when he entered Islam, thereby causing all of his good works to come to nought. If someone who has remained a polytheist wages war on Muslims, he may either be killed, released unconditionally if he has been taken captive, pardoned, or exchanged for Muslim captives, whereas nothing of the kind is possible for the apostate. And, in fact, the difference between the two is significant. Nevertheless, although the apostate who does nothing but change his individual beliefs has violated a right due to God, he has nevertheless not violated the rights of the community. Consequently, God alone has the right to punish the apostate in the life to come for what he has done. If, on the other hand, such a person wages war on the community, it is the right of the community to punish him for the aggression he has committed against it.

The Ḥanbalī School

Ibn Qudāmah summarizes the Ḥanbalī view on apostates as follows: "The statement, 'Carry out the divinely ordained punishments' does not deal with the death penalty for apostasy, since the apostate is killed for his unbelief, not as a divinely ordained punishment." Ibn Qudāmah mentions the details of the Ḥanbalī position on this matter, expounding the evidence in favor of killing the apostate, specifying who is to be punished for this crime, and defining the apostate as someone who has retreated from the religion of Islam to a state of unbelief. He then quotes the hadith. "If anyone changes his religion, put him to death." Supporting it with what he refers to as the consensus among those possessed of knowledge, he says:

> Those possessed of knowledge are in unanimous agreement concerning the necessity of killing the apostate. This has been narrated on the authority of Abū Bakr, ʿUmar, ʿUthmān, ʿAlī, Muʿādh, Abū Mūsā, Ibn ʿAbbās, Khālid, and others, and no opposing views have been mentioned. Hence, there was a consensus on this matter.

He then adds:

> Any rational adult who apostatizes from Islam, man or woman, is to be invited back to Islam for a period of three days, and pressure is to be applied to the person concerned. If the person returns, [his or her repentance is to be accepted], and if not, he or she is to be killed.[15]

This, then, is a summary of the positions taken by the four Sunni schools of Islamic jurisprudence. Some of these positions reveal a clear confusion between apostasy in the political sense, and apostasy in the sense of a change in personal belief and creed. Moreover, the differences among these schools over most details relating to this matter serve as clear evidence of the nonexistence of an explicit text which, in keeping with the principles of Islamic jurisprudence, will support the claim that there is a divinely prescribed death penalty for apostasy. The positions advocated by many Muslim jurists contain allusions to interests relating to the security of the state and society and the protection of the society's internal front based on the link which, as we have seen, is assumed to exist between apostasy and the act of waging war on the Muslim community and/or state.

The Imamite School

The Imamite Shia school holds that there are two types of apostate:

an apostate who was born into Islam, and an apostate who had previously converted to Islam from another religion. The first type is to be put to death immediately and not given any opportunity to repent. If the person takes the initiative to repent, his repentance is not to be accepted; hence, he is not allowed to enter Islam again. As for the second type of apostate, he is to be given an opportunity to repent; if he repents, his repentance will be accepted, and if not, he is to be killed. In the case of a woman, she is not to be killed, but imprisoned instead.

Adherents of this school do not view apostasy as a crime for which there is a divinely prescribed penalty; instead, they classify it among the crimes for which there are discretionary punishments.[16] In their view, any punishment which is referred to explicitly in the Qur'an is referred to as a *ḥadd*, or divinely prescribed punishment, while everything else is referred to as a discretionary punishment (*ta'zīz*). Al-Ḥillī lists six crimes for which there are divinely prescribed punishments, namely, adultery and fornication, false accusation of adultery or fornication, drinking alcoholic beverages, theft and highway robbery. As for crimes for which there are discretionary punishments, he lists them as *al-baghī*, apostasy, bestiality, and the commission of other forbidden acts.

The Zahirite School*

The Zahirite school states that apostasy is a crime for which there is a divinely prescribed punishment, and it is treated in the 'book of divinely prescribed punishments' in Ibn Ḥazm's *al-Muḥalla*.[17] Ibn Ḥazm states:

> If it is confirmed concerning someone that he is a Muslim who has disassociated himself from every religion but the religion of Islam, after which it is confirmed that he has left Islam for Christianity, Judaism, some other religion, or no religion at all, people have differing rulings on such a case. Some hold that such a person should not be given any opportunity to repent, while others maintain that he should be given such an opportunity. Some draw a distinction between those who keep their apostasy a secret and those who make

it public, while some draw a distinction between an apostate who had been born a Muslim, and someone who became a Muslim after being an unbeliever, then apostatized.

Ibn Ḥazm presents the various views on numerous issues relating to apostasy, such as giving the apostate an opportunity to repent, how many opportunities should be given, and over what period of time. He then discusses these views and concludes that according to the Zahirites, an apostate must choose between returning to Islam and dying by the sword. Every Qur'anic verse Ibn Ḥazm perceives as challenging the view which he and his fellow Zahirites hold, he explains away in such a manner that it has no more claim on them. When he comes to the Qur'anic verse that declares, "There shall be no coercion in matters of faith," he claims that it does not mean what it appears to mean, and that none of the leading Muslim scholars has differed with this view. This is – or so Ibn Ḥazm claims – because the Ummah agrees unanimously on the necessity of forcing an apostate to return to his religion. In fact, he goes so far as to claim that scholars have supported only one of two possible verdicts concerning the divine declaration, "There shall be no coercion in matters of faith": (1) that it has been abrogated, and (2) that it applies only to specific people. He claims that this statement has been abrogated because until the end of his life, the Messenger of God insisted that the pagan Arabs either embrace Islam or die by the sword. How, then, asks Ibn Ḥazm, can it be claimed that "There shall be no coercion in matters of faith" when the pagan Arabs were given a choice between Islam and the sword?

As for the claim that the Qur'anic pronouncement, "There shall be no coercion in matters of faith" applies only to certain people – that is, to Jews and Christians – Ibn Ḥazm discusses it at great length. With regard to the hypocrites, Ibn Ḥazm maintains that the Prophet did not know for certain that the hypocrites had reverted to unbelief, or that those whose hypocrisy the Prophet discovered immediately declared their repentance. In discussing this matter, Ibn Ḥazm exhibits an inconsistency that is not customary of him. In the course of discussing the subject of the hypocrites, he says, for example, that whoever believes that the Messenger of God would not have killed those of his Companions whom he had the duty to kill is himself an unbeliever whose life and property may be taken with impunity, since such a person has attributed to the Prophet both falsehood and disobedience to God.

This study does not list in detail all the things said and discussed by Ibn Ḥazm in this connection, since he contradicts himself at more than one point. Anyone who is familiar with Ibn Ḥazm and the breadth of his knowledge is bound to be astonished at the intransigent stance he takes on this issue, a stance he bases on interpretations of numerous Qur'anic verses and hadiths which, had they been put forward by someone else, he would have rejected out of hand in his usual abrupt manner. Hence, readers who would like to see for themselves the manner in which he deals with this topic and the confusion in which he embroils himself in connection with many issues may refer to Part XIII of his book, *al-Muḥallā*.

The Zaydite School*

In his book entitled, *al-Baḥr al-Zakhkhār*, Aḥmad ibn Yaḥyā ibn al-Murtaḍā (d. 850 AH/1058 CE) entitles one of his chapters, "The Chapter on Apostasy and the Killing of Apostates." He also includes a section in which he states that its divinely prescribed punishment is death. Holding to the inclusive sense of the hadith, "If anyone changes his religion, put him to death," he maintains that a woman who apostatizes must be killed just as a man must be. He views it as a duty to give the apostate the opportunity to repent before the death penalty is carried out; however, he also quotes the opposing view that it is not obligatory, but rather, simply recommended that an apostate be given the opportunity to repent. In addition, he quotes the view that if an apostate denies or repudiates his apostasy, this is to be viewed as a form of repentance that will preserve his life, as is the performance of ritual prayer in a non-Muslim land ('the abode of war').[18]

It may be clearly seen from the remaining details cited by those of this school that they look upon apostasy as a declaration of war on the apostate's Muslim nation, if not in actual fact, then in potentiality.[19]

The Ibāḍī School*

Differing little from the other juristic schools, the author of *al-Nīl wa Shifā' al-ʿAlīl* and its commentator stipulate that "the apostate is to be put to death if he or she does not repent." The book's commentator then lists the views of the other schools on the matter of whether the apostate is to be given an opportunity to repent, and on the punishment to be meted out to a woman apostate. In the course of this discussion, he seems to indicate that the *Ibāḍī* school, in addition to holding that both male and female apostates must be put to death, rules out giving the apostate an opportunity to repent, and does not recognize an apostate's repentance even if it occurs.

The author mentions the killing of the apostate before his mention of *ḥirābah*, that is, armed rebellion and highway robbery, then follows this with the statement [that the apostate to whom the death penalty applies is], "a combatant and highway robber who has stolen others' wealth and murdered, and who has been captured."[20]

From what has been said thus far, it will be clear that the Qur'an and the Sunnah affirm freedom of belief, enshrining it as a Qur'anic axiom that is beyond all doubt. As for the confusion observed in scholars' manner of dealing with this matter, it has resulted from numerous causes. One such cause has been an overly broad concept of 'religion' which encompasses the legal system and the need to apply it to all citizens without regard for their differing beliefs. Another is people's having confused a change in one's beliefs with the act of altering the pillars of the religion itself, or the tendency to associate a change in belief with enmity and hostility toward the Muslim Ummah and community such that the apostate becomes an enemy combatant who threatens the interests, security and well-being of his nation.

Islam is founded on a basic principle, namely, the unity of humankind: that all people were created from a single soul and that all people originate from Adam, who was taken from the earth. The

Qur'an acknowledges the many types of differences which distinguish people from one another, including differences in belief. Hence, it declares that those who wish to believe, may believe, while those who wish to disbelieve, may disbelieve. The Prophet forbade Muslims even so much as to think of coercing people into faith, for God had said to him:

> ...had thy Sustainer so willed, all those who live on earth would surely have attained to faith, all of them; dost thou, then, think that thou couldst compel people to believe...? (10:99)

> ...thou canst by no means force them [to believe...]. (50:45)

> Thou canst not compel them [to believe]. (88:22)

> [Say, O Muhammad,] "I have been bidden to worship the Sustainer of this City – Him who has made it sacred, and unto whom all things belong; and I have been bidden to be of those who surrender themselves to Him, and to convey this Qur'an [to the world]." Whoever, therefore, chooses to follow the right path, follows it but for his own good; and if any wills to go astray, say [unto him], "I am only a warner." (27:91–92)

> But if they turn away [from thee, O Prophet, know that] We have not sent thee to be their keeper: thou art not bound to do more than deliver the message [entrusted to thee]. (42:48)

All of this confirms unequivocally that freedom of belief is protected and preserved in the Qur'an. Moreover, given that this is the stance of the Qur'an, it is likewise the stance of the Sunnah. The Qur'an makes clear that the punishment for a change in belief is one that will take effect in the life to come, while the Sunnah likewise makes clear that although a change in belief unaccompanied by anything else may have been interpreted to imply hostility against the Ummah and as a threat to its citizens and interests, there is, nevertheless, no prescribed punishment for it in this earthly life. Rather, the penalty for it pertains to the afterlife alone, since in such a case, it touches exclusively upon a right that belongs to the Creator, and it is He who will collect His due, as it were, in the abode of eternity. And God knows best.

6

MUSLIM SCHOLARS WHO HAVE BEEN ACCUSED OF APOSTASY

In this chapter a selected set of cases will be cited to draw attention to the ways in which some rulers during certain periods of our history have exploited this 'punishment' – a punishment for which there are no grounds – by transforming it into a weapon which they could brandish in the faces of their opponents. Such opponents included prominent scholars who had resisted certain tyrants and, in an attempt to rein in their despotic, absolute powers, had exhorted them, commanded them and prohibited them. In response, however, such despots became even more oppressive, unsheathing over these scholars' necks the very swords which they (the scholars) had placed in their rulers' hands.

The Muslim nation has never discovered the mechanism and tools needed to implement the kind of mutual consultation that God required in the most definitive manner of the Prophet and of the Muslim community after his death. Some God-fearing scholars attempted to perform, albeit to a modest extent, the function that mutual consultation could have performed. However, most rulers unleashed every weapon at their disposal to silence such voices, few though they were, and despite the fact that such scholars' aim was to prevent themselves, the Muslim nation and its tyrannical rulers from being plunged into the abyss of authoritarianism. These scholars took the stances they did in the hope of divine pardon, and in the hope that their listeners would turn back to God in reverence and fear. Yet, how could these tyrants have understood such a thing? And if they had understood it, how could they have tolerated it?

Throughout Islamic history, scholars have sought to make themselves into a force that could stand on a par with those in authority and act as a kind of rear guard. Hence, they have interpreted the Qur'anic phrase, *ūlī al-amr* ('those entrusted with authority') to mean both rulers and scholars. With the end of the era of the rightly guided caliphs – who had combined political vision with authority, the ability to draw sound conclusions from the Qur'an and the Sunnah, and the will to discern what would serve the common good through mutual consultation and all other means at their disposal – scholars were keen not to allow those in power to manage the nation's affairs alone. However, these ignorant rulers, who had been brought to power by tribal coups and family feuds, wasted no time in isolating godly scholars and banning them from their midst. In their place, they surrounded themselves with opportunists, profiteers, poets and panegyrists who found in this type of ruler a means to the achievement of their own ends and the gratification of their own lusts and ambitions.

As scholars with a spiritual vision were thus excluded from participation in public affairs, a kind of individualism of the ruling elite was consecrated and solidified. And as governors and rulers surrounded themselves with corrupt scholars, they gave themselves freer and freer rein to rule as tyrannically as their hearts desired. In the process, they suffered no lack of eulogists and yes-men from among their poets and scholars of ill-repute, who were more than willing to laud them for whatever they happened to do and even entice them into doing more. When these rulers' decadence had reached its nadir, some of them began to view the words, 'Fear God!' as evidence of disrespect for the sultan and as a slur on the prestige of his position. Indeed, they looked upon such an exhortation as an affront to 'God's shadow on earth,' and one ruler had the audacity to say, "If anyone should say, 'Fear God!' I shall have off with his head!"[1] It should come as no surprise then, that some of these sovereigns found in what they referred to as 'the divinely prescribed punishment for apostasy' a sharp sword by means of which they could cut out people's tongues, so to speak, and terrorize their opponents. Later this chapter will examine a number of examples of reform-minded scholars, opposition leaders within governments, orators, mystics, philosophers, as well as leaders of sects in whose faces this weapon was brandished.

Over the course of its history, the Muslim community has witnessed numerous afflictions as a result of disunity, disagreements, disregard for the Qur'an and the living example of the Prophet, and a trend toward dissociating the Qur'an from the Sunnah rather than recognizing the vital link that binds one to the other. Add to this the trend to separate the Qur'an and the Sunnah from jurisprudence; Islamic doctrine from Islamic law and the jurisprudence of earlier scholars from the jurisprudence of later ones, as well as a tendency to view the writings of the founding imams (Abū Ḥanīfah, Aḥmad ibn Ḥanbal, al-Shāfiʿī and Imam Mālik) as though they were on a par with the words addressed to us by the Lawgiver himself.[2] The implication of this latter trend, of course, is that, like the Qur'an and the Sunnah, juristic writings are governed by principles such as opposition,* equilibrium,* abrogation, and the like.

In pursuing such divisions, Muslims have followed in the footsteps of Jews and Christians who have "forgotten much of what they had been told to bear in mind" and broken their solemn covenant with God. Concerning such people God declares:

> Then, for having broken their solemn pledge, We rejected them and caused their hearts to harden – [so that now] they distort the meaning of the [revealed] words, taking them out of their context; and they have forgotten much of what they had been told to bear in mind; and from all but a few of them thou wilt always experience treachery. But pardon them, and forbear; verily, God loves the doers of good. And [likewise,] from those who say, "Behold, we are Christians," We have accepted a solemn pledge; and they, too, have forgotten much of what they had been told to bear in mind – wherefor We have given rise among them to enmity and hatred [to last] until Resurrection Day. And in time God will cause them to understand what they have contrived (5:13–14).

Hardness of heart has caused some Muslims to rush to accuse fellow Muslims of being unbelievers – and even to declare that they should be put to death – for no reason but that they happen to disagree with them on some points. However, all of the criminal, corrupt phenomena witnessed among Muslim sects, groups, movements, blocs and parties are simply a natural outcome of having "forgotten much of what they had been told to bear in mind," and of disregarding the things that bring people's hearts together, foremost among which is an unflagging commitment to the Qur'an. People such as these God leaves to their own devices, allowing enmity, hatred, divisions and discord to grow up among them. And once this situation develops, people's hearts will never be united unless they come to their senses and return to the fundamental reality that brought them together in the first place, namely, the Qur'an with its unchanging truth.

From the time the Muslim community abandoned the Qur'an and was overcome by confusion and error, its unity was lost. It began with the uprising that took place in the days of the third Caliph and led to his martyrdom, then continued with the sedition and intrigue that attended the Battle of the Camel and events at Ṣiffīn, followed by the emergence of sects and differing schools of jurisprudence and the succession of uprisings and conflicts between families that aspired to rule: the Umayyads and their foes, the Umayyads and the Abbasids, then the Abbasids and the Alawids. These were followed by the divisions that arose between the Ashᶜarite and Muᶜtazilite scholastic theologians, between literalist and non-literalist interpreters of scripture, Ḥanbalīs and Shāfiᶜīs, Sunnis and Shias, Seljuks and Buwayhids, Ottomans and Safawids, and on up to the innumerable conflicts that plague us in modern times between Sunni and Shia, Sufi and Salafi, the Salafis and the rest of the Muslim community, and traditionalists and modernists, not to mention the ongoing struggle among the various Islamic political sects and parties, all of which are colored by excess and the tendency to accuse others of being infidels, apostates, hypocrites, rogues, perverts and what have you. Nor is there any end in sight to this anomalous state of affairs, the reason being, quite simply, that people continue to ignore the primary foundation on which the unity of the Muslim community is based, namely, a commitment to God and His Book.

An overview of the phenomenon of accusing others of apostasy and unbelief yields a long list of victims that spans all of Islamic history and that continues to grow, since people have yet to return to a commitment to the Qur'an. The cases listed below are thus a mere fraction of the total, since presenting them all would fill entire volumes.

(1) When, with the help of the Abbasid Caliph Ma'mūn, the Muʿtazilites rose to positions of power and influence, they declared their view that the Qur'an is a created entity, arguing that if we claim that the Qur'an is eternal in its capacity as one of the divine attributes, this could lead to the claim that there is more than one eternal being, which is what led to the kind of idolatry into which the Christians fell when they declared Jesus Christ divine in his capacity as God's Word. It then happened that non-Muʿtazilite scholars who did not share this view of the Qur'an – foremost among whom was Imam Aḥmad ibn Ḥanbal – became victims of a persecution which continued for eighteen years, and which spanned the caliphates of Ma'mūn, his brother al-Muʿtaṣim, and al-Wāthiq. This ordeal only came to an end under the Caliph al-Mutawakkil, whose era witnessed the establishment of what was known as the *ahl al-Sunnah wa al-jamāʿah* movement. At this point, the tables were turned on the Muʿtazilites, who were now subjected to persecution at the hands of those they themselves had abused during their years in power.

One of the most prominent figures to be executed during the Muʿtazilite 'inquisition' was an imam by the name of Aḥmad ibn Naṣr al-Khuzāʿī, who was no less knowledgeable, venerable or steadfast in his faith than Imam Aḥmad ibn Ḥanbal. Historians of that time period have recorded fragments of the trial to which Imam al-Khuzāʿī was subjected during the caliphate of al-Wāthiq. Ibn al-Khuzāʿī states in his history, for example, that "Aḥmad ibn Naṣr al-Khuzāʿī was brought before the Caliph al-Wāthiq on a Saturday, in the beginning of Ramadan, 231 AH/845 CE. Al-Wāthiq: 'What do say about the Qur'an?' Al-Khuzāʿī: 'It is the word of God!' Al-Wāthiq:

'Is it created?' Al-Khuzāʿi: 'It is the word of God!' Al-Wāthiq: 'Will you see your Lord on the Day of Resurrection?' Al-Khuzāʿi: 'This is what the account says.' Al-Wāthiq: 'And is He immanent such as to be seen as a creature is seen?' Al-Khuzāʿī: 'It is the word of God!' Al-Wāthiq: 'Even though it is finite, visible, concrete and occupies space?' Then he added, 'I do not believe in a Lord with attributes such as these!'

The Caliph then looked around at the Muʿtazilite shaykhs and asked, 'What do you say about him?' Judge ʿAbd al-Raḥmān ibn Isḥāq, said, 'Let him be executed!' And his verdict was echoed by the other jurists in attendance. Ibn Abī Dāwūd, the Muʿtazilites' leading scholar at that time, then appeared, not wanting to see al-Khuzāʿī put to death, and said, 'O Commander of the Faithful, here is an elderly man, who may be infirm, and who may not be thinking clearly anymore. Let his case be postponed, and let him be given an opportunity to repent.'

In reply, the Caliph said, 'All I see before me is someone who proclaims and propagates unbelief.' Al-Wāthiq then called for *al-ṣamṣāmah*, that is, the sword of ʿUmar ibn Maʿdī Karib, saying, 'Let no one rise with me, for I am counting my steps toward this infidel who worships a lord which we do not worship, and whose description we do not recognize!' Ordering that a leather mat be brought forth, the caliph sat al-Khuzāʿī on top of it with his hands and feet in shackles. He gave orders for his neck to be pulled taut with a rope and for him to be stretched out, then walked over to him and cut off his head. He issued instructions for Aḥmad's head to be taken to Baghdad and be set up on the East side of the city for several days, then on the Western side for several more days. From his ear they hung a piece of paper which read, 'In the name of God, the most Gracious, the most Merciful: This is the head of Aḥmad ibn Naṣr ibn Mālik, who was called upon by God's servant, Imam Hārūn al-Wāthiq Billāh, the Commander of the Faithful, to declare that the Qur'an is created and to deny any similarity [between it and the uncreated God]. However, he stubbornly refused, so God has sent him to His hellfire.'"

Aḥmad ibn Naṣr's head remained suspended in Baghdad and his body suspended in Samurrā' for a number of days, after which his head and his body were brought together, and he was buried.

(2) *Abū Ḥayyān al-Tawḥīdī*: ʿAlī ibn Muḥammad ibn al-ʿAbbās, was a scholastic theologian and Sufi whose biography was recorded by Ibn al-Subkī[3] and others. According to Abū Ḥayyān's biographers, Minister al-Muhallabī summoned him in order to put him to death; however, he disappeared, and died in hiding. Al-Dhahabī[4] criticized Abū Ḥayyān, branding him as someone with bad doctrine who deserved to be put to death. However, Ibn al-Subkī came to his defense, noting al-Dhahabī's "unspoken hatred for Sufism." He then continued, saying, "As for me, I have yet to find anything in Abū Ḥayyān which justifies such slander against him. I have read many things that he has written, and all I have found is evidence that he was a strong-willed man who held his contemporaries in some contempt. However, this does not provide sufficient reason for such an attack on him."

Al-Dhahabī also held Abū Ḥayyān responsible for another negative phenomenon, namely, that the reputations of those who were placed under scrutiny by a ruler were likely to come under attack. Such an attack, in its turn, would lead another group of scholars to support their arrest and execution, thereby making it look as though the ruler was simply carrying out the legal decisions issued by those possessed of knowledge. However, it was the ruler, and not scholars, who took the initiative in such situations to persecute and condemn the innocent.[5]

(3) *Muḥammad ibn ʿAbd al-Karīm ibn Aḥmad* (Abū al-Fatḥ) – most commonly known as al-Shahrastānī and author of the book, *al-Milal wa al-Niḥal* – was accused of being well-disposed toward Ismaelite* Shiism. He was also described as having confused beliefs and sympathizing with the unorthodox and atheistic. Ibn al-Subkī denied the validity of all these accusations, which would likely have led to al-Shahrastānī's demise if it had not been for his many supporters, who were familiar with his virtue and the soundness of his beliefs.[6]

(4) *Muḥammad ibn ʿAlī ibn al-Ḥasan ibn ʿAlī al-Mayānajī* (Abū al-Maʿālī), ibn Abī Bakr, a native of Khorasan, had been dubbed 'the judges' eye.' Al-Samʿānī wrote concerning him that he was "one of the most virtuous men of his generation, a man of proverbial intelligence and integrity." He was an upright jurist, an eloquent poet, a man with refined sensibilities and a love for Sufism to whom people would come to receive his blessing. However, there was rivalry between him and Abū al-Qāsim, the government minister. The latter drew up a report on him in which he cited obscene expressions from Abū al-Maʿālī's writings. According to Ibn al-Subkī, a group of scholars wrote a statement declaring that he should be put to death. Then he adds, "May God keep us from giving our pens free rein concerning matters of life and death unless we have looked into them with the greatest of care, and from hastily issuing legal opinions declaring that someone should be put to death!" Be that as it may, al-Shahrastānī was arrested by the aforementioned minister and taken to Baghdad in chains. Ibn al-Subkī states, "I saw a letter that he had written from Baghdad to his companions in Hamadhān and which, had it been read in the presence of mighty boulders, would have caused them to shatter from pity and grief." Abū al-Maʿālī was then sent back to Hamadhān and crucified there on Wednesday, 7 Jumādā al-Ākhirah, 525 AH/1130 CE. When he was brought forward to be crucified, he recited the words of God, "...those who are bent on wrongdoing will in time come to know how evil a turn their destinies are bound to take!" (26:227).[7]

(5) *Al-Kiyāharrāsī*, a colleague and fellow student of al-Ghazālī's, taught in numerous schools. When it was rumored that he shared the views of the Ismaelite Shiites, he was summoned and nearly put to death. However, some Ashʿarites came to his defense, saying that the person to whom the accusation applied was not al-Kiyāharrāsī the Ashʿarite, but, rather, the proprietor of Alamut Fortress, Ibn al-Ṣabāḥ, who was a Batinite* Ismaelite who likewise had been dubbed 'al-Kiyā.' Al-Kiyāharrāsī held numerous debates with Ḥanbalī scholars of his time, and it may have been some of his opponents who spread the rumors that nearly led to his demise.[8]

(6) *Abū Naṣr Manṣūr ibn ʿAlī ibn ʿIrāq al-Jaʿdī*, a resident of the city of Mansurah in the region of Khawārizm, was a well-to-do and hospitable man. There were times when he would host up to one thousand guests in a single night, honoring them and taking care of their riding animals for them. When the Sultan Abū al-Qāsim Maḥmūd visited al-Khawārizm, even he stayed at Abū Naṣr's house as his guest, and was received together with his soldiers, their carriages, and their horses. However, when the sultan saw Abū Naṣr's financial capacity, his self-sufficiency and the people's love for him, he accused him of holding wrong beliefs on the pretext that he had not seen a single mosque on his property despite its vast size, and despite the fact that the city of Mansurah was famed for being the site of no fewer than 12,000 mosques! Not even Abū Naṣr's hospitality toward the sultan and the services he had offered him were sufficient to win him a reprieve. Consequently, in 408 AH/1017 CE, the sultan issued orders for Abū Naṣr to be crucified along with others against whom he had leveled the same accusation.

(7) *Ibrāhīm ibn ʿUmar ibn Ḥasan ibn Ribāṭ ibn ʿAlī ibn Abī Bakr al-Biqāʿī*: Burhān al-Dīn, authored a Qur'anic commentary entitled, *Naẓm al-Durar fī Tanāsub al-Āyāt wa al-Suwar* in which he quoted from the Old and New Testaments. As a result, he was attacked by other scholars of his day, who stirred up the rulers against him and accused him of being an unbeliever, then brought a case against him before a Mālikī judge. The Mālikī judge wanted to declare him an unbeliever and sentence him to death; however, Burhān al-Dīn was delivered by the intercession of certain scholars and judges who testified to his Islamic faith, as a result of which the Mālikī judge refrained from having him executed.[9]

(8) *Ibn al-Abbār al-Andalusī* was imprisoned and executed toward the end of 660 AH/1261 CE.[10]

(9) *Aḥmad ibn Ibrāhīm Abū Jaʿfar al-Andalusī*, a grammarian who had memorized the Qur'an in its entirety (627 AH/1229 CE – 708 AH/1308 CE), was described by his contemporaries as a

trustworthy man who promoted what was good and beneficial and sought to prevent what was evil and harmful, and who worked to suppress destructive religious innovations. He was venerated by the common folk and the elite alike; however, he was persecuted and exiled from his homeland.[11]

(10) *Ṣadaqah ibn al-Ḥusayn Abū al-Faraj ibn al-Ḥaddād al-Baghdādī al-Ḥanbalī*, who worked as a copyist and a divider of inheritances, was accused of holding incorrect doctrinal beliefs due to his philosophical leanings. He was the object of scathing criticism by Ibn al-Jawzī due to disagreements between the two men; however, he was highly praised by others, including the hadith scholar of Baghdad, al-Muḥibb ibn al-Najjār in his *History*, where he wrote, "He has written high-quality books on the principles of the religion, and has compiled a history in which he makes mention of events and deaths."[12]

(11) *Ibn Zarqūn*, a leading Mālikī scholar: *Abū al-Ḥusayn Muḥammad*, son of the great imam, Abū ʿAbd Allāh Muḥammad Saʿīd ibn Aḥmad al-Anṣārī al-Ashbīlī, excelled in the field of Islamic jurisprudence and wrote a book entitled, *al-Muʿallā fī al-Radd ʿalā al-Muḥallā*. The ruler of Andalusia and Morocco at that time was a man by the name of Yūsuf ibn Yaʿqūb, a Zahirite thinker who obliged people to take all jurisprudence from the Qur'an and the Sunnah after the manner of the Zahirite school. He went to such extremes in this approach that he forbade people to read about marginal legal questions concerning which various points of view are allowed. Hence, when the sultan discovered that Ibn Zarqūn and another scholar had been reading about such questions, he imprisoned them and burned their books.[13]

(12) *'Al-Sayf'*, that is, *Sayf al-Dīn ʿAlī ibn Abī ʿAlī ibn Muḥammad ibn Sālim al-Taghlabī al-Aẓmidī*, was first an adherent of the Ḥanbalī school, then of the Shāfiʿī school. Sibṭ ibn al-Jawzī describes him in *Mir'āt al-Zamān* (8:691), saying, "He was unsurpassed among his peers in the knowledge of the Qur'an and the

Sunnah and in scholastic theology. At the same time, he was a tenderhearted man who could easily be moved to tears. However, he was hated by all of King ᶜĀdil's sons for his widely acclaimed knowledge of logic and the foundational Qur'anic sciences. He was then expelled from his teaching position at al-ᶜAzīziyyah by al-Ashraf, who issued an edict in the schools according to which anyone who taught the writings of the philosophers or mentioned anything other than Qur'anic commentaries and jurisprudence would be exiled. After this, al-Sayf was accused of apostasy in Cairo, fled to the Levant, and remained confined to his house thereafter until he died."

(13) *Kunayz* was a servant of the Caliph al-Muntaṣir Billāh ibn al-Mutawakkil. When his master died, Kunayz went to Egypt, where he lived for some time, defending his school of jurisprudence and debating with Mālikīs. He then went to teach jurisprudence in Damascus from a Shāfiᶜī point of view. Eventually he was brought before Aḥmad ibn Ṭūlūn by a number of Mālikīs, who claimed that he was a spy who had come from Baghdad. Ibn Ṭūlūn then put him in prison, where he remained for seven years until Ibn Ṭūlūn's death, at which time he was released and went to Alexandria, then to the Levant.[14]

(14) Most commonly known as *Lisān al-Dīn ibn al-Khaṭīb, Muḥammad ibn ᶜAbd Allāh ibn Saᶜīd ibn ᶜAbd Allāh ibn Saᶜīd ibn ᶜAlī ibn Aḥmad al-Salmānī* was originally from Cordoba (d. 776 AH/1374 CE). He excelled in the fields of medicine, logic and mathematics and surpassed his peers in poetry as well. The Sultan of Marrakech, Muḥammad ibn Abū al-Ḥajjāj, elevated him to a position of such power that he eventually took over sole management of the kingdom's affairs. This development produced rancor among a number of Lisān al-Dīn's contemporaries, who brought him before the sultan, who in turn gave them permission to bring suit against him before the Governor's Council. He was convicted of being a *zindīq*, sentenced to death and imprisoned, after which he was found strangled in his cell. The night after he was buried, his body was found burned at the edge of his grave. Lisān al-Dīn's murder and the

subsequent mutilation of his body serve as evidence of the grave errors that have been committed by some rulers, who have handed Muslims over to execution without a shred of legitimate evidence against them.[15]

(15) *Ṣadr al-Dīn ibn al-Wakīl ibn al-Muraḥḥal* (d. 716 AH/1316 CE): *Muḥammad ibn ʿUmar ibn ʿAlī ibn ʿAbd al-Ṣamad ibn ʿAṭiyyah ibn Aḥmad al-Umawī*, was a highly intelligent young man with an exceptional capacity for memorization. His abilities were so outstanding that he was qualified to issue legal opinions by the time he was twenty years old. His numerous enviers concocted charges against him and brought him before Judge Sulaymān, a Ḥanbalī. However, Judge Sulaymān ruled that Ṣadr al-Dīn was a Muslim with sound doctrine, absolved him of any discretionary punishment, and ruled that he should retain his posts. Subsequently, his foes plotted against him again, this time by bringing him before Sultan al-Nāṣir, who removed him from all his teaching posts. Eventually, however, the sultan caught wind of what Ṣadr al-Dīn's enemies had been trying to do, as a result of which he appointed him to numerous posts and his fame spread far and wide. His writings include the book entitled, *al-Ashbāh wa al-Naẓā'ir*.[16]

(16) The venerable *Imam Abū al-Ḥajjāj Jamāl al-Dīn al-Mizzī* (d. 744 AH/1343 CE), who had memorized the Qur'an in its entirety, was also known as Yūsuf ibn al-Zakī ʿAbd al-Raḥmān ibn Yūsuf ibn ʿAbd al-Malik. A master of the Arabic language with a profound knowledge of the hadith sciences, he began teaching at Dār al-Ḥadīth al-Ashrafiyyah. Ibn Taymiyyah wrote about him, saying, "From the time the institution was established, no one who taught there more admirably fulfilled the conditions set by the person who had endowed it." As for al-Dhahabī, he writes, "Never have I encountered anyone in this field who has memorized more than he." He once debated the Shāfiʿīs in defense of Ibn Taymiyyah, as a result of which the Shāfiʿīs brought his case before a Shāfiʿī judge, who ordered him imprisoned, then released him and instructed his deputy to announce that whoever openly challenged Islamic doctrines

should be put to death. His written works include, *Tahdhīb al-Kamāl* and *Kitāb al-Aṭrāf*.[17]

The names listed here are but a drop in the bucket. A search in the books devoted to recording the biographies of Muslim scholars and the history of the Muslim nation would unearth untold numbers of stories of scholars, mystics and jurists who were persecuted, exiled and accused of apostasy, atheism, and deviation from the religion. The real reasons behind what they suffered, of course, lie in the fact that they had crossed this or that ruler or had adopted views and teachings that conflicted with those favored by those in power and by scholars of ill repute. However, if people hold fast to the Qur'an and refuse to depart in any way from what is stated therein, they will strengthen the Muslim community and the religion it professes and prevent it from suffering the painful fates to which it continues to be subjected. And God knows best.

CONCLUSION

THIS, THEN, IS THE ISSUE OF APOSTASY as viewed from the perspective of the Qur'an, the Sunnah, and the writings of Muslim jurists over the ages. In light of the foregoing study, it is clear that according to the Qur'an, the Sunnah and Islamic jurisprudence rooted therein, human beings are too dignified and too dear to God for Him to grant them moral responsibility, then rob them of the freedom to make their own decisions. On the contrary, the essence of the trust human beings have been assigned, and on the basis of which they merit the task of being God's vicegerents on earth, rests on complete, unadulterated freedom of choice:

> There shall be no compulsion in matters of faith. (2:256)
>
> Thou canst not compel them [to believe]. (88:22)
>
> ...thou canst by no means force them [to believe in it]. (50:45)
>
> ...thy duty is no more than to deliver the message; and the reckoning is Ours. (13:40)
>
> ...dost thou, then, think that thou couldst compel people to believe...? (10:99)
>
> Say, "The truth [has now come] from your Sustainer: Let, then, him who wills, believe in it, and let him who wills, reject it." (18:29)

It would be impossible for the Qur'an to affirm human beings' freedom of choice in more than two hundred verses, then punish those who exercise this freedom with such a stern penalty, particularly when they have done nothing to hurt anyone but themselves.

It has likewise become clear through the course of this study that the Muslim jurists who affirmed the death penalty for apostasy generally did so based on the fact that, in the ages in which they lived, apostasy in the sense of a change in personal beliefs was frequently the result of a comprehensive shift away from allegiance to the Muslim community and rejection of its associated systems, laws and culture. This being the case, disbelief in the religion was viewed as tantamount to a total rejection of everything upon which the Muslim community was founded. However, if apostasy could have been seen as nothing but a change in personal belief, whether total or partial, unaccompanied by other crimes, it would not have been possible for them to support this penalty. Moreover, an examination of the evidence upon which these jurists based their conclusions leads to the certainty that the law of mercy and amelioration which the Prophet brought is too sublime a law to impose an earthly penalty of any kind – much less execution – for the exercise of the very freedom it is designed to preserve.

This study has aimed at providing a model for much-needed, serious studies devoted to the review of the Islamic heritage by Muslims themselves. Otherwise, it will remain vulnerable to the ignorant and those who have no patience for serious academic research. This task has been undertaken at a time filled with complexities which are known to all, and under circumstances colored by a worldwide hegemony founded on values, be they liberal, secular or other, that stand in respects opposed to those of Islam. The author's purpose has not been to empower those who seek to exploit the state of weakness, poverty, ignorance, illness and oppression that prevails in the Muslim community in order to entice people to think ill of their religion, its doctrines, and its sublime law. On the contrary, the aim has been to bolster Muslims' faith in the justness of their law and in the purposefulness of every ruling to which it gives rise. The author wants to help them to see that the law of Islam is not one that imposes hardship or undue restrictions. Rather, it is a law of compassion which is open to the entire world and which has the capacity not only to accommodate any civilization or culture on earth, but, in addition, to transcend its relativity and inadequacies, thereby confirming, elevating and refining it. When a true understanding of the intents and higher values of the Qur'an and the Sunnah begins to spread, this will constitute a source of strength of the sort that can never come from mere bigotry and a blind rush to defend Islam; instead, it will provide Muslims with the tool of an informed, purposeful awareness that commands the respect of Islam's foes and detractors.

NOTES

INTRODUCTION

1. An asterisk following a term indicates that it can be found in the Glossary of Terms [translator's note].

CHAPTER ONE

1. It appears that Berlesconi did win some votes in this way. However, despite whatever gains he made through this ploy, he still lost the election!
2. Dr. Muhammad Abd Allah Darraz mentions numerous meanings of the concept of 'religion', and faults dictionaries for their failure to include the manifold and subtle nuances of this concept. Dr. Darraz highlights the contributions made by various dictionaries, listing definitions he has gleaned from the writings of a variety of scholars, then uses them to construct the concept based on its conventional usage; he concludes that neither the notion of belief nor that of submission fully captures the reality represented by the concept of 'religion'. Rather, this concept is broader than either or both of these two notions. For more detail on this topic, see his book, *Al-Dīn: Buḥūth Mumahhadah li Dirāsat Tārīkh al-Adyān* (Kuwait: Dār al-Qalam, 1990), pp. 27–45.

   To trace this concept and the developments it has undergone based on the classics of our Islamic heritage, one would be well advised to begin with Muqātil ibn Sulaymān al-Balkhī (d. 150 AH/757 CE), who wrote the oldest extant commentary on the Qur'an and its vocabulary. Al-Balkhī attributes five distinct meanings to the word 'religion' (*dīn*). [In discussing the first two meanings] he states, "The word *dīn* may be explained in terms of five different meanings. One of these meanings is the affirmation of the oneness of God *(al-tawḥīd)*; this is based on God's words, 'Behold, the only [true] religion (*al-dīn*) in the sight of God is [man's] self-surrender unto Him' (3:19). That is to say: the affirmation of God's oneness is, in the sight of God, man's self-surrender to Him. Similarly God states, '...so worship God, sincere in thy faith in Him alone (*mukhliṣan lahu al-dīn)*' (39:2); that is to say, 'sincere in thy affirmation of God's oneness.' As for the second meaning, it is that of judgment (*al-ḥisāb*), as God states in the opening chapter of the Qur'an, 'Lord of the Day of Judgment (*māliki yawm al-dīn*)' (1:4). God likewise asks on the tongue of an unbeliever whether, 'after we have died and become mere dust and bones we shall, forsooth, be brought to judgment (*annanā la madīnūn*)?' (37:53)." See Muqātil bin Sulaymān, *al-Ashbāh wa al-Naẓā'ir* (Beirut: Dār al-Kutub al-ʿIlmiyyah, 2002).

3. See Muhammad Rashid Rida, *Tafsīr al-Manār* (Beirut: Dār al-Maʿrifah, 1984), 1:55. See also Sayyid Quṭb, *Fī Ẓilāl al-Qur'ān*, 11th Edn. (Cairo: Dār al-Shurūq, 1985), 1:24, and Abu al-Aʿla al-Mawdudi, *al-Muṣṭalaḥāt al-Arbaʿah fī al-Qur'ān*, 5th Edn. (Kuwait, Dār al-Qalam, 1993), pp. 116–130.
4. When the term 'the reformers' or 'the leaders of the reform movement' is used in such a context, those referred to include Jamal al-Din al-Afghani (d. 1897 CE), for whom comprehensive biographical information may be found in *Khāṭirāt ʿan Jamāl al-Dīn al-Afghānī* by Muhammad Basha al-Makhzumi, *Jamāl al-Dīn al-Afghānī al-Muftarā ʿalayhi* by Muhsin Abd al-Hamid, and the introduction to *Al-Aʿmāl al-Kāmilah li Jamāl al-Dīn al-Afghānī* by Muhammad Amarah. Also referred to by the aforementioned appellations is Muhammad Abduh (d. 1905 CE), who served as Mufti of Egypt in his day, and of whom a number of biographies have been written, the most important of which are the biography by Rashid Rida, Abduh's student and publisher of his scholarly works, and Muhammad Amarah's introduction to his complete works. The third figure referred to by the aforementioned appellation is Rashid Rida (d. 1935 CE), editor of *Tafsīr al-Manār* and publisher of *Majallat al-Manār*. Among the numerous biographies of Rashid Rida are *Ārā' Siyāsiyyah li Rashīd Riḍā* by Wajih Kawtharani, *Al-Gharb fī Naẓar Rashīd Riḍā* and *Al-Jāmiʿah al-Islāmiyyah* by Fahd al-Shawabikah. And lastly we have al-Kawakibi (d. 1902 CE), author of *Umm al-Qurā* and *Ṭabā'iʿ al-Istibdād*. There is a sharp division over the correct assessment of these figures and their roles. However, no one could fail to recognize the importance and centrality of the marks they left on the trajectory of the Muslim Ummah and on shaping the mindset of the Arab elite in the 19th Century and the first decades of the 20th Century.
5. See Mahmud Shaltut, *Al-Islām ʿAqīdah wa Sharīʿah*, 18th Edn. (Cairo: Dār al-Shurūq, 2001), p. 281.
6. Freedom is looked upon as the highest of all Western values, second to none. It is the mainstay of liberalism and the foundation of democracy. As for Islam, its governing values are: affirmation of the oneness of God (*al-tawḥīd*), purification (*al-tazkiyah*), and development, prosperity and civilization (*al-ʿumrān*). Islam also grants a place of priority to justice, with freedom

placed lower on the scale. This is an essential distinction to which careful thought needs to be given. This study has noted a large number of juristic concessions which – since the time when contemporary Western civilization began knocking on Muslim doors and confronting them with its challenges – have been made by venerable scholars by not adhering to a comprehensive view of the recognized juristic schools or the positions held by the majority of Muslim jurists and by adopting, instead, abandoned or irregular positions, or positions that had been imported from the outside, as it were, and adjusting their legal arguments and rulings to fit them. And Muslim scholars continue to do the very same thing. However, such practices cannot be viewed as a kind of renewal unless they emerge from the crisis of thought in which they find themselves and base their rulings on the Qur'anic approach to renewal.

7. The term *ḥadd* is rendered for the most part in the course of this translation as 'legally prescribed punishment' [translator's note].
8. *Lisān al-Qur'ān wa ᶜArabiyyatuhu* (Cairo: Dār al-Shurūq al-Dawliyyah, forthcoming).
9. Once in 2:187, six times in 2:229–230, and twice in 65:1 [translator's note].
10. The practice of *ẓihār*, as described in verses 2–3 of the same surah (Surah 58), involves a husband's separating himself unlawfully from his wife by saying to her, "Thou art as unlawful to me as my mother" [translator's note].
11. See verse 3 of the same surah [translator's note].
12. See *Al-Mawsūᶜah al-Fiqhiyyah* (Kuwait, Ministry of Religious Endowments and Islamic Affairs, 1983), vol. 17, p. 129.
13. Ibid.
14. The Prophet did not compose a commentary on the Qur'an in the conventional sense of this term, as some have claimed that he did. There is a small number of specific verses from the Qur'an whose interpretation he was taught by the Angel Gabriel, upon him be peace. In addition to these explanations, the Messenger of God has left behind his lived example in word and deed (his Sunnah). However, Sunnah is one thing, and interpretation another. If the Messenger of God had interpreted all the verses in the Qur'an in the conventional sense of the word 'interpret', it would not have been permissible for anyone to interpret them in any way other than the way in which he himself interpreted them, and all of those interpreters and commentators, including the Companions and their immediate successors on whose authority so many traditions have been handed down relating to the Qur'an's meanings, would have placed themselves at risk of disobeying the Prophet himself. Besides, one may ask: Of what use is the command to reflect and contemplate if the one on whom the Qur'anic revelation was bestowed has interpreted it in its entirety? And if he had done so, how could scholars of jurisprudence, both those who

interpret texts according to their literal sense and those who engage in ijtihad, have recorded so many points of view and teachings based on their own independent interpretations of the Qur'an? Some of these scholars used to derive scores – nay, hundreds – of questions and points from a single verse! There is a vast difference, then, between 'Sunnah' and 'interpretation'. The Sunnah of the Messenger of God is the sum total of the things he said, did and affirmed, and which serve as applications and clarifications of the Qur'an; however, they are not termed 'interpretations' in the conventional sense. And God knows best.

CHAPTER TWO

1. Al-Rāghib al-Iṣfahānī, *Al-Mufradāt fī Gharīb al-Qur'ān* (Beirut: Dār al-Maᶜrifah, 1986), pp. 192–193.
2. See Ibn Manẓūr, *Lisān al-ᶜArab* (Beirut: Dār Iḥyā' al-Turāth al-ᶜArabī, 1993).
3. For this reason, Muslim jurists have stated expressly that a Muslim husband is not permitted to try to persuade his non-Muslim wife to embrace Islam. Nor is he permitted to undermine her religion or to draw comparisons between Islam and her religion in such a way as to demonstrate Islam's superiority over her religion, since all such things are viewed as means of pressuring her and coercing her into conversion.
4. Those who helped and supported the Prophet in Madinah after his emigration there.
5. Muhammad Rashid Rida, *Tafsīr al-Manār* (Beirut: Dār al-Maᶜārif, 1973), 1:117 and 3:36; and Muhammad Izzat Darwazah, *al-Tafsīr al-Ḥadīth*, 7:383.
6. Al-Bukhārī states that it took place before the Battle of Uḥud, which is known for a certainty to have taken place in the month of Shawwāl in the year 3 AH.
7. *Tafsīr al-Manār*, 3:36–37.

CHAPTER THREE

1. A piece written by the author for the "Qur'anic Studies" series, forthcoming from Maktabat al-Shurūq al-Dawliyyah in Cairo, discusses the notion of abrogation and how this idea, or rather, fallacious theory, made its way into our intellectual circles.
2. That is, to Madinah.
3. Al-Mutaqqī al-Hindī, *Kanz al-ᶜUmmāl* (Aleppo: Maktabat al-Turāth al-Islāmī, 1979), vol. 1, Section 3, the chapter entitled, *Dhamm Akhlāq al-Jāhiliyyah* ("In Criticism of Pre-Islamic Morals").
4. Al-Bayhaqī relates on the authority of al-Zuhrī and ᶜUrwah that the Prophet was taken on his night journey one year before his departure for Madinah. In

discussing the time at which the five daily prayers were instituted, al-Ḥākim relates that it took place sixteen months before the Hijrah; this view is also supported by Ibn Kathīr in *al-Bidāyah wa al-Nihāyah* (3:108–109). Al-Zamakhsharī makes mention in *al-Kashshāf* (2:37) of the sharp disagreement that exists over the dating of the Night Journey, including the view that it took place one year before the Hijrah, as well as the peculiar view that it took place before his call to prophethood!

5. Abū Muḥammad ʿAbd al-Malik ibn Hishām ibn Ayyūb al-Ḥimyarī (218 AH/833 CE), *al-Sīrah al-Nabawiyyah*, 1st Edn., edited by al-Saqqa, al-Abyari and Shalabi, 1st Edn. (Beirut: Dār Iḥyā' al-Turāth al-ʿArabī, 1994), 2:12.
6. Abū ʿAbd Allāh al-Ḥākim al-Nīsābūrī (405 AH/1014 CE), *al-Mustadrak ʿalā al-Ṣaḥīḥayn*, edited by Sami ibn Muhammad al-Salamah (Aleppo: Maktab al-Maṭbūʿāt al-Islāmiyyah), *Kitāb Maʿrifat al-Ṣaḥābah* ("the book on the knowledge of the Companions"), 3:62.
7. Abū al-Fidā' Ismāʿīl ibn ʿUmar ibn Kathīr al-Qurashī al-Dimashqī (774 AH/1372 CE), *Tafsīr al-Qur'ān al-ʿAẓīm*, 1st Edn. (Riyadh: Dār Ṭībah, 1997), 5:28. He states that its chain of transmission is sound.
8. Abū Jaʿfar Muḥammad ibn Muḥammad ibn Jarīr al-Ṭabarī (310 AH/922 CE), *Jāmiʿ al-Bayān fī Ta'wīl Āy al-Qur'ān* (Beirut: Dār al-Jabal, no date), 8:76.
9. Ibid., 8:87.
10. Ibn Hishām, *al-Sīrah al-Nabawiyyah*, 1:260.
11. Muḥammad ibn Saʿd ibn Manīʿ al-Hāshimī al-Baṣrī (230 AH/844 CE), *al-Ṭabaqāt al-Kubrā*, 1st Edn., edited by Muhammad Abd al-Qadir Ata (Beirut: Dār al-Kutub al-ʿIlmiyyah, 1990), 8:77; Aḥmad ibn Yaḥyā al-Balādhurī (279 AH/892 CE), *Ansāb al-Ashrāf*, edited by Muhammad Hamid Allah (Cairo: Dār al-Maʿārif, 1991), 1:199; Abū al-Ḥasan ʿAlī ibn Muḥammad al-Jazarī (630 AH/1232 CE), *Usd al-Ghābah fī Maʿrifat al-Ṣaḥābah*, edited by Muawwad and Abd al-Mawjud (Beirut: Dār al-Kutub al-ʿIlmiyyah, 1994), 7:116. All of these writers agree that ʿUbayd Allāh ibn Jaḥsh apostatized, as no one has included his biography among those of the Prophet's Companions. Rather, he is mentioned in the biography of Ramlah Bint Sufyān (Umm Ḥabībah). What is amazing in connection with this man is that he was one of four who had refused to bow down to idols prior to the advent of Islam. He was among those who had gone in search of the true religion, the religion of Abraham, upon him be peace. In this connection we have an account related by Ibn Hishām on the authority of Ibn Isḥāq, who says, "Once, in celebration of a holiday of theirs, the Qurayshites had gathered around an idol which they venerated, and they were circumambulating it and offering it sacrifices. This was a holiday they celebrated once every year. However, four of them broke away from the gathering, saying to each other, 'Be loyal friends and

companions to one another, and let each of us guard the other's secret.' And to this all of them agreed. The four men referred to were Waraqah ibn Nawfal, ʿUbayd Allāh ibn Jaḥsh, ʿUthmān ibn al-Ḥuwayrith, and Zayd ibn ʿAmr ibn Nufayl. They said to one another, 'You know – and God is our witness – that our people are in error! They have failed to follow the religion of their father Abraham. This stone around which we circumambulate neither hears nor sees, and it has power neither to harm nor to bring benefit! O people, seek a [true] religion for yourselves, for you, verily, are in error.' Thereupon they scattered throughout the lands in search of the true, unsullied religion of Abraham." (Ibn Hishām, *al-Sīrah al-Nabawiyyah*, 1:259) The question that comes to mind is: How could a discerning person who had refused to worship idols, then found in Islam the truth he had searched for so long, possibly turn away from it and go back to the state he had been in before?

12. That is, Abū ʿUbaydah Maʿmar ibn al-Muthannā al-Taymī al-Baṣrī al-Naḥwī; al-Dhahabī, *Siyar Aʿlām al-Nubalā'* (Beirut: Mu'assasat al-Risālah, 1988), 9:445.
13. Al-Balādhurī, *Ansāb al-Ashrāf*, 1:219. With the exception of Abū ʿUbaydah Maʿmar al-Naḥwī, none of the Companions' biographers mentions that al-Sakrān apostatized after entering Islam and returned to Abyssinia as an apostate. Ibn Saʿd includes biographical information about him in *al-Ṭabaqāt al-Kubrā* (4:154), Ibn al-Athīr al-Jazarī includes him in *Usd al-Ghābah* (2:504), and he is mentioned by all such writers as having been one of the Companions. Al-Balādhurī himself states that the first account is "more accurate and better established," and the same opinion is expressed by others.
14. That is, he used to record the revelations that would come to the Prophet [translator's note].
15. Narrated by al-Bukhārī in *al-Manāqib*, in the section on 'Signs of Prophethood in Islam', No. 3421.
16. Narrated by Muslim in *Ṣifāt al-Munāfiqīn wa Aḥkāmuhum*, No. 2781; a similar hadith is narrated by Aḥmad in *Bāqī Musnad al-Mukthirin min al-Ṣaḥābah*, Nos. 11805, 12991 and 13161, all of which are narrated on the authority of Anas. This man's name is not mentioned in commentaries, nor in writings that deal with obscure names which appear in hadiths' texts or chains of transmission, and all we are told is that he was from the tribe of Banū al-Najjār.
17. Narrated by Abū Dāwūd in *al-Ḥudūd*, or legally prescribed penalties, the section entitled *al-ḥukm fī man irtadd* ("the ruling on those who commit apostasy"), No. 4358; it is narrated by al-Nasā'ī in *taḥrīm al-dam* ("declaring someone's blood to be under protection"), the section entitled *tawbat al-murtadd* ("repentance by an apostate"), No. 4069. The text of the hadith, which

was passed down on the authority of Ibn ʿAbbās, is as follows: "We read in *Sūrah al-Naḥl*, 'As for anyone who denies God after having once attained to faith – and this, to be sure, does not apply to one who does it under duress, the while his heart remains true to his faith, but [only, to] him who willingly opens up his heart to a denial of the truth –: upon all such [falls] God's condemnation, and tremendous suffering awaits them' (16:106). However, God then abrogated this and made an exception to it, saying, 'And yet, behold, thy Sustainer [grants His forgiveness] unto those who forsake the domain of evil after having succumbed to its temptation, and who thenceforth strive hard [in God's cause] and are patient in adversity: behold, after such [repentance] thy Sustainer is indeed Much-Forgiving, a Dispenser of Grace!' (16:110). ʿAbd Allāh ibn Abī Sarḥ, who was over Egypt, used to record for the Messenger of God. However, Satan caused him to stumble, and he joined up with the unbelievers. On the day when Makkah was conquered, the Messenger of God gave instructions that he should be put to death; however, ʿUthmān ibn ʿAffān made a plea on his behalf, in response to which the Messenger of God granted him protection." It is narrated also by al-Ḥākim in *al-Maghāzī*, 3:45. All these accounts are on the authority of Ibn ʿAbbās. See his biography in Ibn Saʿd, *al-Ṭabaqāt al-Kubrā* (7:344) and Ibn al-Athīr al-Jazarī, *Usd al-Ghābah*, 3:260. The complete story may be found in Ibn Hishām, *al-Sīrah al-Nabawiyyah*, 4:57.

18. Al-Balādhurī, *Ansāb al-Ashrāf*, 1:358.
19. Ibn Ḥajar al-ʿAsqalānī, *Fatḥ al-Bārī* (Beirut: Dār al-Kutub al-ʿIlmiyyah, 1992), vol. 12, *Kitāb al-Ḥudūd* ("the book on legally prescribed punishments"), the section dealing with "carrying out the legally prescribed punishments in Islam against the high-born and the lowly."
20. Ibn Saʿd, *al-Ṭabaqāt al-Kubrā*, 2:103 and al-Balādhurī, *Ansāb al-Ashrāf*, 1:357.
21. Ibn Hishām, *al-Sīrah al-Nabawiyyah*, 4:58.
22. That is, the Battle of Banū al-Muṣṭaliq [translator's note].
23. Al-Balādhurī, *Ansāb al-Ashrāf*, 1:358.
24. Ibn Hishām, *al-Sīrah al-Nabawiyyah* (Beirut: Dār al-Fikr li al-Ṭibāʿah wa al-Nashr, 1992), 4:58.
25. Al-Balādhurī, *Ansāb al-Ashrāf* (Cairo: Dār al-Maʿārif, 1978), 1:359–360.
26. The writer of *al-Miṣbāḥ al-Munīr* states concerning the term *qasāmah* (compurgation by oath): "[It is] an oath which is made by the clan of someone who has been slain if they claim that the person has been murdered. It is said, *qutila fulān bi al-qasāmah* if the relatives of someone who has been slain come together and claim that a particular man killed their relative, if they have inconclusive evidence in support of their accusation, and if fifty of these

family members take an oath to the effect that the accused person killed their relative. The individuals who swear to the truth of such an accusation are also referred to as *qasāmah*." Like the word *qasam*, the term *qasāmah* is a verbal noun related to the verb *aqsama*. It also refers to an oath (similar to the verbal noun *ḥalf* relating to the verb *ḥalafa*). It is a means of negation or affirmation which is based on a repeated oath made up to fifty times when someone, a man or a woman, enters a city, village or encampment, shortly after which someone is found murdered without his or her murderer having been identified, and without there being any evidence, presumption, or sign that might lead to the murderer himself, while at the same time, there is a feud or enmity involved. Numerous accounts may be found which explain the origin of *qasāmah* and which indicate its necessity – that is, the need for fifty of the residents of the area in which someone was murdered to swear that they did not kill the person, and that they do not know who killed him or her. Along with this oath, the payment of blood money is required of these individuals in order to finalize the matter or, as we would say today, to close the file and to record the case against an anonymous [accused]. A great deal has been written concerning the term's precise meaning, when it is to be used and on what conditions, and from whom such an oath is valid. For more detail on this theme, see *Badā'iʿ al-Ṣanā'iʿ fī Tartīb al-Sharā'iʿ* (7:231), Ibn Qudāmah, *al-Mughnī* (8:382), *Nihāyat al-Muḥtāj ilā Sharḥ al-Minhāj* (7:387ff.), and al-Mardāwī, *al-Inṣāf* (10:139ff.).

27. Narrated by al-Bukhārī in his chapter on *al-diyyāt* ('blood money'), the section entitled *qasāmah*, No. 6899. Muslim likewise narrates this hadith under "*qasāmah*, those who go to war, retribution and blood money" in the section entitled *ḥukm al-muḥāribīn wa al-murtaddīn* ("the ruling on those who wage war [on the Apostle] and apostates"), No. 1671. It is narrated by al-Nasā'ī in his chapter entitled *taḥrīm al-dam* ("declaring people's blood to be under protection") in the context of his commentary on the verse, "The punishment of those who wage war against Allah and His Messenger, and strive with might and main for mischief through the land is: execution, or crucifixion, or the cutting off of hands and feet from opposite sides, or exile from the land: that is their disgrace in this world, and a heavy punishment is theirs in the Hereafter" (5:33), Nos. 4024–4035. (Yusuf Ali's translation has been used here for this verse in keeping with the author's intent and argument, since Muhammad Asad takes exception to the view that this verse communicates a legal injunction; for his discussion of this point, see Muhammad Asad, *The Message of the Qur'an* (Gibraltar: Dar al-Andalus, 1984), pp. 148–149, Notes 43, 44 and 45 [translator's note].) It is narrated by Abū Dāwūd in his chapter entitled, *al-ḥudūd* ('legally prescribed punishments'), the section entitled *al-Muḥārabah* ("Waging War"), No. 4364.

28. This statement by the author seems to imply that the men not only murdered the shepherd, but mutilated him as well [translator's note].
29. Ibn Ḥazm al-Andalusī, *al-Muḥallā*, 13:141.
30. Although the Arabic phrase *lā ikrāha fī al-dīn* is rendered in English as an injunction – "There shall be no coercion in matters of faith" – it is, in its literal import, a simple statement of fact, and, translated literally, would read, "There is no coercion in matters of faith." It is for this reason that the writer classifies it as a report [translator's note].
31. For commentary on these two verses from *Sūrah al-Tawbah*, see *Tafsīr al-Ṭabarī* (Cairo: Dār al-Maᶜārif, 1988), 14:357–369, where al-Ṭabarī mentions the disagreement among interpreters as to the nature of the 'hard striving' (*jihād*) which God commanded the Prophet to engage in against the hypocrites.
32. The implication here appears to be that at the time when ᶜUmar had sought permission to kill ᶜAbd Allāh ibn Ubayy, the Muslim men referred to here were ᶜAbd Allāh ibn Ubayy's supporters, and not well established in their Islamic faith. Hence, his being put to death would have been a cause of offense to them, and may have caused them to doubt the Prophet's character [translator's note].
33. Ibid., 8:154.
34. Ibn Ḥajar al-ᶜAsqalānī, *Fatḥ al-Bārī* (Beirut: Dār al-Kutub al-ᶜIlmiyyah, 1992), vol. 12, *Kitāb al-Ḥudūd* ("the book on legally prescribed punishments in Islam"), the section on "carrying out the legally prescribed punishments against the high-born and the lowly."
35. Ibn Hishām, *al-Sīrah al-Nabawiyyah*, 3:346.
36. Muḥammad ibn Saᶜd ibn Manīᶜ al-Hāshimī al-Baṣrī, *al-Ṭabaqāt al-Kubrā*, edited by Muhamamd Abd al-Qadir Ata, 1st Edn. (Beirut: Dār al-Kutub al-ᶜIlmiyyah, 1990), 2:74; and Abū Jaᶜfar Muḥammad ibn Jarīr al-Ṭabarī, *Tārīkh al-Umam wa al-Mulūk* (Beirut: Dār al-Kutub al-ᶜIlmiyyah, 1995), 2:122.
37. Ibid., 3:347.
38. Ibid., 3:352.
39. See al-Bayhaqī, *Maᶜrifat al-Sunan wa al-Āthār* (Cairo: Al-Majlis al-Aᶜlā li al-Shu'ūn al-Islāmiyyah, 1969), 12:251.
40. Quoted by al-ᶜAynī in ᶜ*Umdat al-Qārī Sharḥ Ṣaḥīḥ al-Bukhārī* (Beirut: Nashr Muḥammad Amīn, 1979), 11:235.

CHAPTER FOUR

1. See earlier quote by al-ᶜAynī in ᶜ*Umdat al-Qārī Sharḥ Ṣaḥīḥ al-Bukhārī*, 11:235.

2. On the authority of Abū Burdah.
3. In *Irwā' al-Ghalīl fī Takhrīj Aḥādīth Manār al-Sabīl* (Beirut: al-Maktab al-Islāmī, 1979), 8:125, al-Albani states, "[This hadith is] sound according to conditions set by Muslim and al-Bukhārī (al-Bukhārī, No. 6923 and Muslim, *Kitāb al-Imārah* ("The Book on Princely Authority"), 3:1456–1457, which has a similar wording except that it does not include the words, 'whoever reverts....' The hadith indicates that this incident took place during the days of the Prophet; however, it remains to be determined whether he knew of the matter or not. And if he did know of it, we need to determine whether or not he approved this action. There is an account on the authority of Abū Mūsā according to which the Prophet said to him, "Go to Yemen," after which he sent Muʿādh ibn Jabal to Yemen as well. When Muʿādh came to see Abū Mūsā, he threw him a cushion and said, "Sit down and rest...." It then became apparent that there was a man who was bound in Abū Mūsā's presence. "What is this?" asked [Muʿādh]. [Abū Mūsā] replied, "He was a Jew, then he became a Muslim, then he became a Jew again." In response, [Muʿādh] said, "I will not sit down until he has been put to death. This is the decree of God and His Apostle." And he repeated these words three times. He then gave orders for the man to be killed, and he was killed. After the words, "he was killed," Abū Dāwūd adds, "He had been given an opportunity to repent before this." In one account related by Abū Dāwūd we also read, "...for twenty days and nights."
4. Yusuf Ali's translation.
5. See al-Bayhaqī, *Maʿrifat al-Sunan wa al-Āthār* (Cairo: Al-Majlis al-Aʿlā li al-Shu'ūn al-Islāmiyyah, 1969), 12:251.
6. It is a statement the truth of which has been denied by many scholars, and which is discussed by al-Shāṭibī in his book, *al-Muwāfaqāt*.
7. On the authority of ʿAbd al-Raḥmān ibn Muḥammad ibn ʿAbd Allāh ibn ʿAbd al-Qārī, on the authority of his father.
8. On the authority of ʿAbd al-Raḥmān ibn Muḥammad, who quotes Khalaf ibn al-Qāsim on the authority of Ibn Abī al-ʿUqayb on the authority of Ibn Abī Zurʿah on the authority of Aḥmad ibn Khālid on the authority of Muḥammad ibn Isḥāq on the authority of ʿAbd al-Raḥmān ibn Muḥammad ibn ʿAbd Allāh ibn ʿAbd al-Qārī on the authority of his father.
9. On the authority of Dāwūd ibn Abī Hind on the authority of al-Shaʿbī on the authority of Anas ibn Mālik (who also related the hadith having to do with the conquest, and which is mentioned by al-Bayhaqī alone) that they went down to Tustur.
10. By ʿAbd Allāh ibn Rabīʿ ibn ʿAbd Allāh ibn ʿAbd Allāh ibn Muḥammad ibn ʿUthmān ibn ʿAlī ibn ʿAbd al-ʿAzīz ibn al-Ḥajjāj ibn al-Minhāl on the

authority of Ḥammād ibn Salamah on the authority of Dāwūd ibn Abī Hind, on the authority of al-Shaʿbī, on the authority of Anas.

11. See Ibn Ḥazm, *al-Muḥallā* (Cairo: Maktabat al-Jumhūriyyah al-ʿArabiyyah, 1972), Part 13, p. 124.
12. See Note 6 chapter 5.
13. The term Zuṭṭ refers to a Gypsy-like people who originated in Sind (the lower Indus River Valley) [translator's note].
14. Ibn ʿAbd al-Barr was a hadith scholar and jurist who died in the year 463 AH/ 1070 CE.
15. See Ibn Saʿd, *al-Ṭabaqāt al-Kubrā*, edited by Muhammad Abd al-Qadir Ata, 1st Edn. (Beirut: Dār al-Kutub al-ʿIlmiyyah, 1990), 5:219.
16. The chain of narrators includes Abū al-Nuʿmān Muḥammad ibn al-Faḍl, on the authority of Ḥammād ibn Zayd, on the authority of Ayyūb, on the authority of ʿIkrimah.
17. The chain of narrators includes "ʿAffān on the authority of Ḥammād ibn Zayd on the authority of Ayyūb...", after which he relates the story and the hadith.
18. The chain of narrators includes Isḥāq ibn Abī Isrā'īl, on the authority of Sufyān ibn ʿUyaynah and Ḥammād ibn Zayd on the authority of Ayyūb... (yet without mentioning the story).
19. The chain of narrators includes al-Ḥasan ibn Sufyān, on the authority of Muḥammad ibn ʿAbd ibn Ḥisāb, on the authority of Ḥammād ibn Zayd, (after which he mentions both the story and the hadith).
20. The chain of narrators includes Yūsuf, on the authority of Shihāb ibn ʿAbbād, on the authority of Ḥammād ibn Zayd, (after which he mentions the hadith without the story).
21. The chain of narratiors includes Abū Muḥammad ʿAbd Allāh ibn Muḥammad, on the authority of Saʿīd ibn al-Sakan, on the authority of Muḥammad ibn Yūsuf, on the authority of Muḥammad ibn Ismāʿīl al-Bukhārī.
22. The chain of narrators includes Abū al-Ḥusayn ibn al-Faḍl al-Qaṭṭān, on the authority of ʿAbd Allāh ibn Jaʿfar on the authority of Yaʿqūb ibn Sufyān (ḥā'). Another chain includes Abū al-Ḥasan ʿAlī ibn Aḥmad ibn ʿAbdān, on the authority of Aḥmad ibn Sulaymān ibn Ḥarb, on the authority of Ḥammād ibn Zayd...
23. The chain of narrators includes ʿAlī ibn ʿAbd Allāh on the authority of Sufyān on the authority of Ayyūb...
24. Some have denied that there is any *tadlīs* in this chain of narrators based on what is stated explicitly by al-Ḥumaydī in his *Musnad* on the authority of Sufyān based on the hadith related by Ayyūb.

25. That is, ʿAmmār's account, according to which the burning did not take place [translator's note].
26. The chain of narrators includes Saʿīd ibn Naṣr, on the authority of Qāsim ibn Aṣbagh, on the authority of Muḥammad ibn Ismāʿīl al-Tirmidhī, on the authority of al-Ḥumaydī, on the authority of Sufyān, on the authority of Ayyūb, on the authority of ʿIkrimah.
27. The chain of narrators includes Muḥammad ibn al-Ṣabāḥ, on the authority of Sufyān ibn ʿUyaynah on the authority of Ayyūb...
28. The chain of narrators includes Ibn ʿUyaynah on the authority of Ayyūb..."
29. The chain of narrators includes Isḥāq ibn Abī Isrā'īl, on the authority of Sufyān ibn ʿUyaynah and Ḥammād ibn Zayd, on the authority of Ayyūb....
30. The chain of narrators includes Ibn ʿUyaynah on the authority of Ayyūb..." after which he relates both the story and the hadith.
31. The chain of narrators includes Abū ʿAbd Allāh al-Ḥāfiẓ, on the authority of Abū al-ʿAbbās Muḥammad ibn Yaʿqūb, on the authority of al-Rabīʿ ibn Sulaymān, on the authority of al-Shāfiʿī...".
32. The chain of narrators includes Aḥmad ibn ʿAbd Allāh al-Ṣāliḥī and Muḥammad ibn Aḥmad al-ʿĀrif, on the authority of Abū Bakr Aḥmad ibn al-Ḥasan al-Ḥīrī, on the authority of Abū al-ʿAbbās al-Aṣamm (ḥā'), on the authority of ʿAbd al-Wahhāb ibn Muḥammad al-Kisā'ī, on the authority of ʿAbd al-ʿAzīz ibn Aḥmad al-Khallāl, on the authority of Abū al-ʿAbbās al-Aṣamm, on the authority of al-Shāfiʿī..."
33. On the authority of ʿImrān ibn Mūsā, on the authority of ʿAbd al-Wārith, on the authority of Ayyūb, on the authority of ʿIkrimah...
34. Narrators include Muḥammad ibn ʿAbd Allāh ibn al-Mubārak (who is al-Mukharramī), on the authority of Abū Hishām (that is, al-Makhzūmī), on the authority of Wuhayb, on the authority of Ayyūb, on the authority of ʿIkrimah.
35. Narrators include Maḥmūd ibn Ghīlān, on the authority of Muḥammad ibn Bakr, on the authority of Ibn Jurayḥ, on the authority of Ismāʿīl, on the authority of Maʿmar, on the authority of Ayyūb...
36. Narrated by Imam Abū ʿAlī al-Ḥusayn ibn Muḥammad al-Qāḍī on the authority of Abū Ṭāhir al-Zayādī on the authority of Abū Ḥāmid Aḥmad ibn Muḥammad ibn Muḥammad ibn Yaḥyā ibn Bilāl, on the authority of Abū al-Azhar Aḥmad ibn al-Azhar, on the authority of Yazīd ibn Hārūn, on the authority of Saʿīd – that is, al-Jarīrī – on the authority of Ayyūb, on the authority of ʿIkrimah, on the authority of Ibn ʿAbbās..."
37. Narrated by Aḥmad ibn Isḥāq ibn Bahlūl, on the authority of my father, on the authority of Yazīd, on the authority of Saʿīd ibn Abī ʿUrūbah, on the authority of Ayyūb.

38. Narrated by al-Maḥāmilī on the authority of al-Ḥasā'ī on the authority of Yazīd, on the authority of Sa'īd.
39. The chain of narrators include Aḥmad ibn 'Abdah al-Ḍabbī al-Baṣrī, on the authority of 'Abd al-Wahhāb al-Thaqafī, on the authority of Ayyūb, on the authority of 'Ikrimah.
40. The chain of narrators include Aḥmad ibn Ḥanbal, on the authority of Ismā'īl ibn Ibrāhīm ibn Ayyūb, on the authority of 'Ikrimah...
41. The chain includes 'Abd Allāh ibn Muḥammad ibn 'Abd al-Mu'min, on the authority of Muḥammad ibn Bakr, on the authority of Abū Dāwūd.
42. See the aforementioned presentation of these under the heading, "The chain of narrators which includes Ma'mar ibn Rāshid."
43. Narrators include Hilāl ibn al-'Alā' on the authority of Ismā'īl ibn 'Abd Allāh ibn Zurārah, on the authority of 'Abbād ibn al-'Awwām, on the authority of Sa'īd, on the authority of Qatādah, on the authority of Ibn 'Abbās...
44. Narrators include Mūsā ibn 'Abd al-Raḥmān, on the authority of Muḥammad ibn Bishr, on the authority of Sa'īd, on the authority of Qatādah, on the authority of al-Ḥasan.
45. Narrators include Mūsā ibn Hārūn on the authority of Isḥāq ibn Rāhwayh, on the authority of Ibrāhīm ibn al-Ḥakam ibn Abān, on the authority of his father, on the authority of 'Ikrimah, on the authority of Ibn 'Abbās.
46. Narrated by al-Ḥusayn ibn 'Isā, on the authority of 'Abd al-Ṣamad, on the authority of Hishām, on the authority of Qatādah, on the authority of Anas, on the authority of Ibn 'Abbās.
47. Narrated by Muḥammad ibn al-Muthannā, on the authority of 'Abd al-Ṣamad, on the authority of Qatādah, on the authority of Anas, (that 'Alī brought in people belonging to a national group known as the Zuṭṭ who were worshipping an idol, after which he burned them with fire. Ibn 'Abbās states that the Messenger of God said, 'If anyone changes his religion, put him to death.')
48. Narrated by 'Abd al-Ṣamad, on the authority of Hishām ibn Abī 'Abd Allāh, on the authority of Qatādah (whereupon he mentions the story of the Zuṭṭ and the hadith with wording similar to that of al-Nasā'ī).
49. Narrated by Isḥāq on the authority of 'Abd al-Ṣamad...
50. Narrated by Aḥmad ibn al-Ḥasan ibn 'Abd al-Jabbār al-Ṣūfī, on the authority of Yaḥyā ibn Ma'īn, on the authority of 'Abd al-Ṣamad ibn 'Abd al-Wārith, on the authority of Hishām, on the authority of Qatādah, on the authority of Anas ibn Mālik, on the authority of Ibn 'Abbās.
51. Narrated in al-Kabīr (10638) by 'Abd Allāh ibn Aḥmad ibn Ḥanbal, on the authority of Muḥammad ibn Abī Bakr al-Muqaddamī, on the authority of

ʿAbd al-Ṣamad ibn ʿAbd al-Wārith, on the authority of Hishām al-Dastawāʾī, on the authority of Qatādah.

52. Narrated by Abū al-Ḥasan ʿAlī ibn Muḥammad al-Muqrī, on the authority of al-Ḥasan ibn Muḥammad ibn Isḥāq, on the authority of Yūsuf ibn Yaʿqūb, on the authority of Muḥammad ibn Abī Bakr al-Muqaddamī, on the authority of ʿAbd al-Ṣamad.

53. On the authority of ʿAbd al-Raḥmān ibn Sulaymān, on the authority of ʿAbd al-Raḥmān ibn ʿUbayd, on the authority of his father.

54. Based on the chain of narrators which includes ʿAbd Allāh ibn Sharīk al-ʿĀmirī on the authority of his father.

55. Narrated by Dāwūd ibn Muḥammad ibn Ṣāliḥ al-Marwazī, on the authority of Ḥawtharah ibn Ashras, on the authority of Ḥammād ibn Salamah, on the authority of Bahz ibn Ḥakīm, on the authority of his father, on the authority of his grandfather.

56. Al-Haythamī declares its narrators to be trustworthy; it is also related by Abū Ḥafṣ al-Kittānī in part of his hadith (Section 2:141) based on what is mentioned by al-Albani in *Irwāʾ al-Ghalīl* (8:125) without citing its chain of transmission. Instead, he contents himself with al-Haythamī's declaration of confidence, as he generally does in connection with hadiths that he declares reliable.

57. Narrated by Nuʿaym ibn Muḥammad al-Ṣūrī, on the authority of Mūsā ibn Ayyūb al-Nuṣaybī, on the authority of ʿAbd al-Raḥmān ibn al-Ḥasan Abū Masʿūd al-Zajjāj, on the authority of Abū Bakr al-Hudhalī, on the authority of al-Ḥasan and Shahr ibn Ḥawshab, on the authority of ʿĀʾishah.

58. Narrated by Masʿūd ibn Muḥammad al-Ramlī, on the authority of ʿImrān ibn Hārūn, on the authority of ibn Lahīʿah, on the authority of Bukayr ibn ʿAbd Allāh ibn al-Ashbaḥ, on the authority of Sulaymān ibn Yasār, on the authority of Abū Hurayrah.

59. Narrated by Muḥammad ibn ʿAbd Allāh ibn Faḍl, on the authority of Muḥammad ibn Mufaḍḍal, on the authority of ʿUmar ibn ʿAbd al-Wāḥid, on the authority of Ibn Abī Farwah, on the authority of Abū al-Munkadir, on the authority of ʿAṭāʾ ibn Yasār, on the authority of Abū Hurayrah.

60. Narrated by Aḥmad ibn Rushd ibn al-Maṣrī, on the authority of Khālid ibn ʿAbd al-Salām al-Ṣadafī, on the authority of al-Faḍl ibn al-Mukhtār, on the authority of ʿAbd Allāh ibn Mawhib, on the authority of ʿIṣmah ibn Mālik al-Khaṭmī.

61. Narrated by Mālik, on the authority of Nāfiʿ, on the authority of Ibn ʿUmar.

62. Narrated by Mūsā ibn ʿAbd al-Raḥmān, on the authority of Muḥammad ibn Bishr, on the authority of Saʿīd, on the authority of Qatādah, on the authority of al-Ḥasan.

63. "We were informed by al-Ḥusayn ibn Isḥāq al-Tusturī, on the authority of Hawbar ibn Muʿādh, on the authority of Muḥammad ibn Salamah, on the authority of al-Fazārī, on the authority of Makḥūl, on the authority of Ibn Abī Ṭalḥah al-Yaʿmurī, on the authority of Abū Thaʿlabah al-Khushanī, on the authority of Muʿādh ibn Jabal..."
64. 'The four': Al-Tirmidhī, al-Nasā'ī, Ibn Mājah and Abū Dāwūd [translator's note].
65. See, for example, Ibn Jarīr al-Ṭabarī, *Tārīkh al-Umam wa al-Mulūk* (Beirut: Dar al-Kutub al-ʿIlmiyyah, 1995), 2:257ff.; and Ibn al-Athīr, *al-Kāmil fī al-Tārīkh* (Beirut: Dār Ṣādir, 1965), 2:342ff.
66. on the authority of Abū Bakr ibn ʿAyyāsh, on the authority of Abū Ḥusayn, on the authority of Suwayd ibn Ghaflah.

CHAPTER FIVE

1. Verses 72–73.
2. Al-Kāsānī, *Badā'iʿ al-Ṣanā'iʿ fī Tartīb al-Sharā'iʿ* (Cairo: Zakariyyā ʿAlī Yūsuf, 1968), 7:134.
3. Ibid.
4. See, for example, *Badā'iʿ al-Ṣanā'iʿ* by al-Kāsānī, 7:134–140, 7:142 and elsewhere; in *al-Mukhtaṣar fī al-Fiqh* by al-Ṭaḥāwī, the writer's discussion of apostasy is separate from his 'book of divinely prescribed punishments' (*Kitāb al-Ḥudūd*); similarly, in al-Qadduri's *Mukhtaṣar* and his commentary entitled, *al-Lubāb fī Sharḥ al-Kitāb*, *Kitāb al-Ḥudūd* is followed by a series of chapters on various subjects, which is followed in turn by his 'book on matters pertaining to jihad' (*Kitāb al-Siyar*), at the end of which the author discusses dhimmis, that is, non-Muslim subjects of an Islamic state, after which he presents rulings on apostates.
5. See, for example, Shaykh Ullaysh, *Minaḥ al-Jalīl ʿalā Mukhtaṣar al-Shaykh Khalīl* (Cairo: al-Maṭbaʿah al-Amīriyyah, 1294 AH/1877 CE), 4:461–487; al-Ḥaṭṭāb, *Mawāhib al-Jalīl li Sharḥ Mukhtaṣar Khalīl* (Cairo: Maṭbaʿat al-Saʿādah, 1329 AH/1911 CE), 6:279–290; *Al-Kharashī ʿalā Mukhtaṣar Khalīl*, 2nd Edn. (Cairo: al-Maṭbaʿah al-Amīriyyah, 1317 AH/1899 CE), 8:62–74; and *Ḥāshiyat al-Rahūnī alā Sharḥ al-Shaykh ʿAbd al-Bāqī al-Zarqānī*, 1st Edn. (Cairo: al-Maṭbaʿah al-Amīriyyah, 1306 AH/1888 CE), 8:87–115.
6. The Arabic word *zanādiqah* (singular, *zindīq*) gained wide circulation during the Abbasid era and was used to refer to Muslims who had reverted to Mazdaism (more commonly known as Zoroastrianism), since the Mazdians, or Zoroastrians, are said to believe in a book known in Arabic as *zindāqinastā* (English, the Zend-Avesta). Hence, someone who believed in this book was

known as a *zindīq*. Al-Fayyumi notes in *al-Miṣbāḥ al-Munīr* that the word *zindīq* conforms to the same pattern as the word *qindīl* (lamp). Some have said that the word is of Persian origin, but was then Arabized. Quoting Thaʿlab, Ibn al-Jawālīqī states, "A man is referred to as *zandaqī* or a *zindīq* if he is extremely stingy." Quoting someone else he states, "I asked a desert Arab about the word *zindīq* and he replied, 'He is someone who examines matters carefully.'" A common definition of the term *zindīq* is someone who does not adhere to Islamic law and who believes in the eternity of time. Arabs refer to such a person as an atheist (*mulḥid*), that is, someone who challenges the truth of all religions. It has also been said that the *zindīq* is someone who does not believe in an afterlife or in the oneness of the Creator. Al-Qurṭubī, who was a Mālikī, states in his *Tafsīr* (1:200), "The Prophet did not kill the *zanādiqah* who were hypocrites because God Almighty had protected His Prophet's Companions by his (the Prophet's) having established them so firmly that they could not be corrupted by the hypocrites, nor could the hypocrites corrupt their religion; hence, there was no harm in allowing them to live. This is no longer true today, however, because we can no longer be certain that the *zanādiqah* will not corrupt the general populace and the ignorant." This statement serves to confirm that apostasy is not associated with any particular divinely ordained punishment.

7. See previous note on this term.
8. Ibn Rushd, *al-Muqaddimāt* (Cairo: Maṭbaʿat al-Saʿādah, no date), 285–286.
9. Ibn Rushd, *Bidāyat al-Mujtahid wa Nihāyat al-Muqtaṣid* (Cairo: Maktabat al-Kulliyyāt al-Azhariyyah, 1974), 2:259.
10. Imam al-Shāfiʿī, *al-Umm* (Beirut: Dār al-Fikr, 1983), 6:168–184.
11. That is, zakah.
12. Narrated by al-Bukhārī, Part 6, p. 2522, Hadith No. 6484; narrated by Muslim, Part 3, p. 1303, Hadith No. 1676; narrated by the compilers of the remaining *Sunan* thereafter, as well as Aḥmad, al-Ḥākim, al-Dārqutnī, al-Nasā'ī, al-Bayhaqī, and others.
13. Muḥammad ibn Idrīs al-Shāfiʿī, *al-Umm* (Dār al-Maʿrifah, 1990), 6:169.
14. In our study on stoning, we view this as an aggravating circumstance which merits a more severe punishment than that meted out for sexual misconduct by an individual, in whose case it is considered a fall or slip into sin. This latter situation includes the virgin or unmarried person who engages in sexual intercourse, in whose case the person's marital status serves as an extenuating circumstance, as a result of which the Qur'anically specified punishment is flogging.
15. See *al-Mughnī wa al-Sharḥ al-Kabīr* (Cairo, Ṭabʿ al-Manār, 1348 AH/1929 CE), 10:74–83. On pages 80–81, he discusses those who have argued on the

basis of the saying of the Prophet, "Carry out the divinely prescribed punishments." However, Ibn Qudāmah's discussion of apostasy and magic precedes his 'book of divinely prescribed punishments.' Moreover, Ibn Qudāmah himself states clearly on page 77 that al-Nakhʿī, who was a prominent successor of the Prophet's Companions, held the view that the apostate should be given an indefinite period of time to repent; however, he seems not to have noticed al-Nakhʿī's departure from the majority view. He also mentions ʿUmar among those who agreed unanimously on the necessity of killing the apostate; however, it is an established fact that ʿUmar, although he agreed with Abū Bakr on the legitimacy of fighting the apostates who refused to pay zakah, he is widely known to have opposed the killing of an individual apostate who has not waged war on the Muslim community.

This view of ʿUmar's has been recorded by Ibn Ḥazm and others. See *al-Muḥallā* (13:124), where it is mentioned that ʿUmar said, "If I had brought them [the apostates] in, I would have proposed that they return to Islam. If they had repented [I would have accep-ted their repentance], and if they had not, I would have kept them in prison." Numerous traditions passed down by the Companions on ʿUmar's authority to this effect have been referred to above. Hence, Ibn Qudāmah either interpreted what has been narrated on ʿUmar's authority as applying strictly to the matter of encouraging the apostate to repent, and therefore included him among those who agreed on the necessity of putting the apostate to death, or he failed to see in the disagreement voiced by ʿUmar and al-Nakhʿī that which would invalidate the claim to a consensus on this matter.

16. See *Sharāʿiʿ al-Islām* (2:243–261) and *Miftāḥ al-Karāmah fī Sharḥ Qawāʿid al-ʿAllāmah* by Muhammad al-Jawad al-Husayni al-Amili (Egypt Edition, 1326 AH/1908 CE), 8:35–37. Al-Muḥaqqiq al-Ḥillī states clearly that there is no disagreement over the fact that the apostate's repentance is not to be accepted, even if he declares his repentance, seeks refuge in God and appears to be sincere. He then quotes from the book entitled, *al-Khilāf* as stating that there is a consensus concerning the unacceptability of an apostate's repentance. See also Shaykh al-ʿĀmilī (d. 1104 AH/1692 CE), *Wasā'il al-Shīʿah ilā Taḥṣīl Masā'il al-Sharīʿah*, 9:544, the sections concerning apostates.
17. Ibn Ḥazm, *al-Muḥallā* (Beirut: Al-Maktab al-Tijārī li al-Ṭibāʿah wa al-Nashr, 1969), 13:3.
18. Aḥmad ibn Yaḥyā ibn al-Murtaḍā, *al-Baḥr al-Zakhkhār al-Jāmiʿ li Madhāhib ʿUlamā' al-Amṣār* (Beirut: Mu'assasat al-Risālah, 1982) 6:422ff.
19. Ibid., 6:423.
20. Muḥammad Ibn Yūsuf, Aṭṭafayyish, *al-Nīl wa Shifā' al-ʿAlīl* (Jeddah: Maktabat al-Irshād, 1985), 14:786.

CHAPTER SIX

1. This statement, or something similar thereto, is said to have been uttered by ʿAbd al-Malik ibn Marwān, Abū Jaʿfar al-Manṣūr and others of their ilk.
2. The term 'lawgiver' in such a context may refer either to God or to the Prophet [translator's note].
3. ʿAbd al-Wahhāb ibn ʿAlī al-Subkī, *Ṭabaqāt al-Shāfiʿiyyah al-Kubrā,* edited by al-Tannaji and al-Hilw, 1st Edn. (Cairo: Maṭbaʿat al-Bābī al-Ḥalabī, 1964), 5:286.
4. Muḥammad ibn Aḥmad al-Dhahabī, *Siyar Aʿlām al-Nubalā'*, edited by al-Arnaut and al-Araqsusi, 1st Edn. (Beirut: al-Risālah, 1983), 17:119.
5. For a discussion of the soundness of al-Tawḥīdī's doctrine and the groundlessness of the accusations leveled against him, see Dr. Muhammad Hammam, "Abu Hayyan al-Tawhidi Naqidan," Unpublished doctoral dissertation, Al-Qaḍi ʿIyad University, Marrekesh, Morocco, 1998.
6. For a more detailed statement of Ibn al-Subkī's defense of al-Shahrastānī, see *Ṭabaqāt al-Shāfiʿiyyah al-Kubrā*, 4:79ff.
7. Ibn al-Subkī, *Ṭabaqāt al-Shāfiʿiyyah*, 4:236–237.
8. Ibid., 7:231.
9. Muḥammad ibn ʿAlī al-Shawkānī, *al-Badr al-Ṭāliʿ bi Maḥāsini Man Baʿd al-Qarn al-Sābiʿ*, 1st Edn. (Cairo: Maṭbaʿat al-Saʿādah, 1348 AH/1929 CE), 1:19.
10. Al-Dhahabī, *Siyar Aʿlām al-Nubalā'*, 23:337.
11. Al-Shawkānī, *al-Badr al-Ṭāliʿ*, 1:33.
12. Al-Dhahabī, *Siyar Aʿlām al-Nubalā'*, 21:66–67.
13. Ibid., 22:311.
14. Ibn al-Subkī, *Ṭabaqāt al-Shāfiʿiyyah*, 2:79.
15. Al-Shawkānī, *al-Badr al-Ṭāliʿ*, 2:191.
16. Ibid., 2:234.
17. Ibid., 2:353.

BIBLIOGRAPHY

Abd al-Fattah, Sayf al-Din, "Al-Janib al-Siyasi li Mafhum al-Ikhtiyar lada al-Muʿtazilah," unpublished M.S. thesis presented to the Faculty of Economics and Political Science, University of Cairo, 1982.

Al-Albani, Muhammad Nasr al-Din, *Irwāʾ al-Ghalīl fī Takhrīj Aḥādīth Manār al-Sabīl* (Beirut: Al-Maktab al-Islāmī, 1979).

Ali, Muhammad Kurd, *Umarāʾ al-Bayān* (Cairo: Lajnat al-Taʾlīf wa al-Tarjamah wa al-Nashr, 1976).

Alalwani, Taha Jabir, *Lisān al-Qurʾān wa ʿArabiyyatuhu* (Cairo: Maktabat al-Shurūq al-Dawliyyah, forthcoming).

______, *Maqāṣid al-Sharīʿah* (Beirut: Dār al-Hādī, 2003).

______, *Naḥwa Manhajiyyah Maʿrifiyyah Qurʾāniyyah* (Beirut: Dār al-Hādī, 2004).

Al-Amili, Muhammad al-Jawad al-Husayni, *Miftāḥ al-Karāmah fī Sharḥ Qawāʿid al-ʿAllāmah*, 1st Edn. (Cairo: 1908).

Al-ʿAsqalānī, ibn Ḥajar, *Fatḥ al-Bārī Sharḥ Ṣaḥīḥ al-Bukhārī* (Beirut: Dār al-Kutub al-ʿIlmiyyah, 1992).

Attafayyish, Muhammad ibn Yusuf, *Al-Nīl wa Shifāʾ al-ʿAlīl* (Jeddah: Maktabah al-Irshād, 1985).

Al-ʿAynī, Badr al-Dīn Maḥmūd ibn Aḥmad *ʿUmdat al-Qārī Sharḥ Ṣaḥīh al-Bukhārī* (Beirut: Nashr Muhammad Amin, 1979).

______, *Wasāʾil al-Shīʿah ilā Taḥṣīl Masāʾil al-Sharīʿah*, (Beirut: Muʾassasat āl al-Bayt li Iḥyāʾ al-Turāth, 1993).

Al-Balādhurī, Aḥmad ibn Yaḥyā, *Ansāb al-Ashrāf*, ed. Hamid Allah, Muhammad (Cairo: Dār al-Maʿārif, 1991).

Al-Bayhaqī, Aḥmad ibn al-Ḥusayn, *Shuʿab al-Īmān* (Cairo: Al-Maṭbaʿah al-Munīriyyah, 1938).

______, *Maʿrifat al-Sunan wa al-Āthār* (Cairo: Higher Council of Islamic Affairs (al-Majlis al-Aʿlā li al-Shuʾūn al-Islāmiyyah), 1969).

Darraz, Muhammad Abd Allah, *Al-Dīn: Buḥūth Mumahhadah li Dirāsat Tārīkh al-Adyān* (Kuwait: Dār al-Qalam, 1990).

Darwazah, Muhammad Izzat, *Al-Qur'ān wa al-Mubashshirūn*, 3rd Edn. (Al-Maktab al-Islāmī, 1979).

Al-Dhahabī, Muhammad ibn Ahmad, *Siyar A^clām al-Nubalā'*, 1st Edn., ed. Al-Arnaut wa al-Araqsusi (Beirut: Mu'asssat al-Risālah, 1983).

Al-Dhahabī, Muhammad Husayn, *Al-Isrā'īliyyāt fī al-Tafsīr wa al-Ḥadīth* (Cairo: Majma^c al-Buḥūth al-Islāmiyyah, 1971).

Al-Ghannushi, Rashid, *Al-Ḥurriyyāt al-^cĀmmah fī al-Dawlah al-Islāmiyyah* (Beirut: Markaz Dirāsāt al-Waḥdah al-^cArabiyyah, 1995).

_____, *Ḥuqūq al-Muwāṭanah: Ḥuqūq Ghayr al-Muslim fī al-Mujtama^c al-Islāmī* (Herdon, Virginia: The International Institute of Islamic Thought, 1993).

Hammam, Muhammad, "Abu Hayyan al-Tawhidi Naqidan," unpublished Ph.D. thesis. Al-Qāḍī ^cIyād University, Marrakesh, Morocco, 1998.

Al-Hattab, Muhammad ibn Muhammad al-Maghribi, *Mawāhib al-Jalīl li Sharḥ Mukhtaṣar Khalīl* (Cairo: Maṭba^cat al-Sa^cādah, 1911).

Al-Ḥillī, Abū al-Qāsim Najm al-Dīn Ja^cfar, *Sharā'i^c al-Islām fī Masā'il al-Ḥalāl wa al-Ḥarām*, 2nd Edn., with commentary by al-Sayyid Sadiq al-Shirazi (Beirut: Markaz al-Rasūl al-A^cẓam, 1998).

Al-Ḥumaydī, ^cAbd Allāh ibn al-Zubayr, *Musnad al-Ḥumaydī* (Beirut: 1980).

Ibn al-Athīr, ^cIzz al-Dīn Abū al-Ḥasan, *Al-Kāmil fī al-Tārīkh*, (Beirut: Dār Ṣādir, 1965).

Ibn Ḥazm ^cAlī ibn Aḥmad, *Al-Muḥallā* (Beirut: Al-Maktab al-Tijārī li al-Ṭibā^cah wa al-Nashr, 1969).

Ibn Hishām, Abū Muḥammad ^cAbd al-Malik, *Al-Sīrah al-Nabawiyyah*, 1st Edn., ed. al-Abyari, Ibrahim (Beirut: Dār Iḥyā' al-Turāth al-^cArabī, 1994).

_____, *Al-Sīrah al-Nabawiyyah* (Beirut: Dār al-Fikr li al-Ṭibā^cah wa al-Nashr, 1992).

_____. *Al-Sīrah al-Nabawiyyah*. eds. al-Qutb, Muhammad Ali and Baltah, Muhammad al-Dali (Beirut: Al-Maktabah al-^cAṣriyyah, 1998).

Ibn Kathīr, Abū al-Fidā' Ismā^cīl ibn ^cUmar, *Tafsīr al-Qur'ān al-^cAẓīm*, 1st Edn. (Riyadh: Dār Ṭībah, 1997).

Ibn Khaldūn, ^cAbd al-Raḥmān, *Al-Muqaddimah*, ed. Wafi, Ali Abd al-Wahid (Cairo: Nahḍat Miṣr li al-Ṭibā^cah wa al-Nashr wa al-Tawzī^c, 2004).

Ibn Manẓūr, Muḥammad ibn Mukarram, *Lisān al-^cArab* (Beirut: Dār Iḥyā' al-Turāth al-^cArabī, 1993).

Ibn al-Mulaqqin, ^cUmar ibn ^cAlī, *Tuḥfat al-Muḥtāj bi Sharḥ al-Minhāj* (Damascus: Dār al-Bashā'ir, 1991).

Ibn Qudāmah, Muwaffaq al-Dīn ^cAbd Allāh ibn Aḥmad, *Al-Mughnī*, ed. al-Hilw, Abd al-Fattah. (Cairo: Dār Hājar, 1986).

_____, *Al-Mughnī* wa al-Sharḥ al-Kabīr (Cairo: Ṭab^c al-Manār, 1929).

Ibn Rushd, Muḥammad ibn Aḥmad ibn Muḥammad, *Al-Muqaddimāt* (Cairo: Maṭbaʿah al-Saʿādah, n. d).

______, *Bidāyat al-Mujtahid wa Nihāyat al-Muqtaṣid* (Cairo: Maktabah al-Kulliyāt al-Azhariyyah, 1974).

Ibn Saʿd, Muḥammad ibn Manīʿ al-Hāshimī al-Baṣrī, *Al-Ṭabaqāt al-Kubrā*, 1st Edn., ed. Ata, Muhammad Abd al-Qadir (Beirut: Dār al-Kutub al-ʿIlmiyyah, 1990).

Al-ʿIrāqī, ʿAbd al-Raḥmān ibn al-Ḥusayn, *Takhrīj al-ʿIrāqī ʿalā Iḥyā' ʿUlūm al-Dīn* (Cairo: Dār al-Shaʿb, 1981).

Al-Iṣfahānī, Abū al-Qāsim al-Ḥusayn ibn Muḥammad, *Al-Mufradāt fī Gharīb al-Qur'ān* (Beirut: Dār al-Maʿrifah, 1986).

Al-Jazarī, Abū al-Ḥasan ʿAlī ibn Muḥammad, *Usd al-Ghābah fī Maʿrifat al-Ṣaḥābah*. eds. Muawwad, Ali and al-Mawjud, Adil Abd (Beirut: Dār al-Kutub al-ʿIlmiyyah, 1994).

Al-Kāsānī, Abū Bakr ibn Masʿūd, *Bada'iʿ al-Ṣanāʿiʿ fī Tartīb al-Sharāʿiʿ* (Cairo: Zakariyya Ali Yusuf, 1968).

Al-Kharashī, Muḥammad ibn ʿAbd Allāh, *Sharḥ Mukhtaṣar Khalīl*, 2nd Edn. (Cairo: Al-Maṭbaʿah al-Amīriyyah, 1899).

Mālik, ibn Anas, *Al-Muwaṭṭa'* (Cairo: Dār al-Shaʿb, n.d).

Al-Mardāwī, ʿAlā' al-Dīn Abū al-Ḥasan ʿAlī ibn Sulaymān, *Al-Inṣāf fī Maʿrifat al-Rājiḥ min al-Khilāf ʿalā Madhhab al-Imām al-Mubajjal Aḥmad ibn Ḥanbal*, 2nd Edn., ed. al-Fiqqi, Muhammad Hamid (Beirut: Dār Iḥyā' al-Turāth al-ʿArabī, 1986).

Al-Mawdudi, Abu al-Aʿla, *Al-Muṣṭalaḥāt al-Arbaʿah fī al-Qur'ān*, 5th Edn. (Kuwait: Dār al-Qalam, 1993).

Al-Mawsūʿah al-Fiqhiyyah (Kuwait: Ministry of Religious Endowments and Islamic Affairs, 1983).

Al-Maydānī, ʿAbd al-Ghanī al-Ghunaymī al-Ḥanafī, *Al-Lubāb fī Sharḥ al-Kitāb*, ed. al-Hamid, Muhammad Muhyi al-Din Abd (Beirut: Al-Maktabah al-ʿIlmiyyah, 1992).

Al-Munāwī, ʿAbd al-Ra'ūf ibn Tāj al-Dīn, *Fayḍ al-Qadīr* (Cairo: Dār al-Maʿrifah, 1972).

Muqātil, ibn Sulaymān, *Al-Ashbāh wa al-Naẓā'ir* (Beirut: Dār al-Kutub al-ʿIlmiyyah, 2002).

Al-Muttaqī al-Hindī, ʿAlī ibn ʿAbd al-Malik, *Kanz al-ʿUmmāl* (Aleppo: Maktabat al-Turāth al-Islāmī, 1979).

Al-Nabhānī, Yūsuf ibn Ismāʿīl, *Al-Fatḥ al-Kabīr* (Damascus: Al-Maktab al-Islāmī, 1970).

Al-Nīsābūrī, Abū ʿAbd Allāh al-Ḥākim, *Al-Mustadrak ʿalā al-Ṣaḥīḥayn*, ed. al-Salamah, Sami ibn Muhammad (Aleppo: Maktab al-Maṭbūʿāt al-Islāmiyyah, 1984).

Al-Qurṭubī, Muḥammad ibn Aḥmad al-Anṣārī, *Al-Jāmiᶜ li Aḥkām al-Qur'ān* (Beirut: Dār al-Kutub al-ᶜIlmiyyah, 1988).

Qutb, Sayyid, *Fī Ẓilāl al-Qur'ān*, 11th Edn. (Cairo: Dār al-Shurūq, 1985).

Al-Rāzī, Fakhr al-Dīn Muḥammad ibn ᶜUmar, *Al-Maḥṣūl fī ᶜIlm Uṣūl al-Fiqh*. ed. al-Alwani, Taha Jabir (Beirut: Mu'assasat al-Risālah, 1994).

Rida, Muhammad Rashid, *Tafsīr al-Manār* (Beirut: Dār al-Maᶜrifah, 1984).

Al-Samurrai, Numan Abd al-Razzaq, *Aḥkām al-Murtadd fī al-Sharīᶜah al-Islāmiyyah* (Riyadh: Dār al-ᶜUlūm, 1983).

Al-Shāfiᶜī, Muḥammad ibn Idrīs, *Al-Umm* (Beirut: Dār al-Fikr, 1983).

______, *Al-Umm* (Beirut: Dār al-Maᶜrifah, 1990).

Shaltut, Mahmud, *Al-Islām ᶜAqīdah wa Sharīᶜah*, 18th Edn. (Cairo: Dār al-Shurūq, 2001).

Al-Shawkānī, Muḥammad ibn ᶜAlī, *Al-Badr al-Ṭāliᶜ bi Maḥāsin Man Baᶜd al-Qarn al-Sābiᶜ*, 1st Edn. (Maṭbaᶜah al-Saᶜādah, 1949).

Al-Subkī, ᶜAbd al-Wahhāb ibn ᶜAlī, *Ṭabaqāt al-Shāfiᶜiyyah al-Kubrā*, 1st Edn., eds. al-Tannaji, Mahmud and al-Hilw, Abd al-Fattah (Cairo: Maṭbaᶜat al-Bābī al-Ḥalabī, 1964).

Al-Ṭabarī, Abū Jaᶜfar Muḥammad ibn Jarīr, *Tārīkh al-Umam wa al-Mulūk* (Beirut: Dār al-Kutub al-ᶜIlmiyyah, 1995).

______, *Jāmiᶜ al-Bayān fī Ta'wīl āy al-Qur'ān* (Beirut: Dār al-Jīl, 1983).

ᶜUllaysh, Muḥammad ibn Aḥmad, *Minaḥ al-Jalīl ᶜalā Mukhtaṣar al-Shaykh Khalīl* (Cairo: Al-Maṭbaᶜah al-Amīriyyah, 1877).

Al-Wazir, Zayd ibn Ali, *Al-Fardiyyah: Baḥth fī Azmat al-Fiqh al-Fardī al-Siyāsī ᶜind al-Muslimīn* (Sanaa: Markaz al-Turāth wa al-Buḥūth al-Yamanī, 2000).

Al-Zamakhsharī, Abū al-Qāsim Jār Allāh Maḥmūd ibn ᶜUmar, *Al-Kashshāf ᶜan Ḥaqā'iq al-Tanzīl wa ᶜUyūn al-Aqāwīl fī Wujūh al-Ta'wīl* (Beirut: Dār al-Maᶜrifah, 1970).

Al-Zarqānī, Muḥammad ibn ᶜAbd al-Bāqī, *Ḥāshiyat al-Rahūnī ᶜalā Sharḥ al-Shaykh al-Zarqānī*, 1st Edn. (Cairo: Al-Maṭbaᶜah al-Amīriyyah, 1888).

GLOSSARY OF TERMS

Sources from which definitions have been taken for this glossary largely include: Qalanji, Muhammad Rawwas, et. al., *Muʿjam Lughat al-Fuqahā'*, English-French-Arabic (Beirut: Dār al-Nafā'is, 1996); Ashraf Taha Abu al-Dhahab, *Al-Muʿjam al-Islāmī: al-Jawānib al-Dīniyyah wa al-Siyāsiyyah wa al-Ijtimāʿiyyah wa al-Iqtiṣādiyyah* (Cairo: Dār al-Shurūq, 2002); Deeb al-Khudrawi, *A Dictionary of Islamic Terms* (Damascus-Beirut: al-Yamamah for Printing and Publishing, 1995).

Athar (plural, *āthār*), or tradition: The account of a statement or action attributed to one of the Companions, as distinguished from words or actions attributed to the Prophet himself.

Baghī: The rebellion of a powerful group against the rightful Muslim ruler based on a particular interpretation of the Qur'an and Sunnah.

Batinite (Arabic, *bāṭinī*, meaning 'secret' or 'hidden'): A term used to describe a number of religious sects which conceal their teachings from outsiders, and who believe that the Qur'an and the Sunnah have both outward, apparent meanings and inward, hidden ones. Another feature of these sects is their belief that those who penetrate to the inward meanings of the Qur'an and the Sunnah are exempt from the requirements of Islamic law. The Ismaelite Shias and the Druze are examples of Batinite sects.

Confirmatory (Arabic, *taqrīrī*): By 'confirmatory', the author is referring to those aspects or parts of the Sunnah which deal not with a specific action or statement of the Prophet himself but, rather, with his affirmation or approval of an action or statement on someone else's part.

Equilibrium (Arabic, *taʿādul*): The existence of two opposing pieces of textual evidence which are equal in weight.

Ibāḍī: The *Ibāḍī*s are a Kharijite sect which agrees with the Sunnis on a large number of points, and which oversaw a state of its own in Morocco from 162 AH/778 CE to 297 AH/909 CE. The *Ibāḍī*s were among the first to record the Prophetic hadiths.

Ijtihad, or independent reasoning: The effort exerted by a suitably qualified scholar of jurisprudence to arrive at an accurate conceptualization of the divine will based on Muslim legal sources (the Qur'an, the Hadith, analogical deduction and consensus) and the means by which to apply this will in a given age and under given circumstances; as such, ijtihad is the effort exerted by such a scholar to derive a legal ruling from Muslim legal sources, and to reach certainty on questions of an ambiguous nature.

Incompletely transmitted hadith: See *Mursal* below.

Ismaelite Shiism: A Batinite Shia sect whose origins are attributed to Ismāʿīl ibn Jaʿfar al-Ṣādiq, who is viewed by the Shias as the Seventh Imam. Its followers hold that they are exempt from the requirements of the law and that the Divine Essence is devoid of attributes; they are also said to believe in reincarnation.

Istifāḍah: A term used to characterize a hadith that has gained wide acceptance in the Muslim community without regard for the number of narrators who passed it down.

Judaica: The term 'Judaica' refers to stories, legends, and beliefs specific to the Jewish tradition which were passed on to Muslim commentators on the Qur'an through Jewish people with whom they were in contact, including some who had embraced Islam.

Muḍṭarib: Confused or disturbed; this word is used to refer to a hadith which has been related by one or more narrators in different and contradictory ways such that the differing accounts cannot be reconciled or harmonized, nor can it be decided which of them should prevail over the others.

Mursal: A term used to describe an incompletely transmitted hadith, namely, one which rests on a chain of authorities that goes no further back than the second generation after the Prophet.

Opposition (Arabic, *taʿāruḍ*): The phenomenon of one text's affirming what another text denies.

Qadyaniyyah (or *Kadianeia*): Followers of this sect, founded by Mirza Ghulam Ahmad (d. 1908), claim to be Muslims. However, they hold that Muhammad was not the seal of the prophets and that revelation is still ongoing.

Solitary Hadith: A solitary hadith (*ḥadīth āḥād*) is a report related by a single person and passed down by one or more chains of narrators, but which does not fulfill the requirements of *tawātur*, (See *tawātur* below.)

Tadlīs: The practice of narrating a hadith on the authority of a contemporary whom the narrator has met, but from whom he did not actually hear the account in question, or whom he has not even met; it also includes the narration of a hadith in such a way that it gives the false impression that it was narrated on the authority of someone other than the actual source of the account.

Tawātur: A term used to describe a report related by more than one person, then handed down by so many separate chains of narrators that it would be impossible for them to have colluded in falsification.

Tradition: See *athar* above.

Ummah: The Muslim community worldwide.

Zahirite (Arabic, *ẓāhirī*, meaning 'literalist': The Zahirite school, founded by Dāwūd ibn ʿAlī al-Iṣbahānī (d. 270 AH/883 CE), insists on understanding texts from the Qur'an and the Sunnah based on their apparent meanings, and opposes attempts to derive underlying meanings or causes therefrom.

Zaydite: The Zaydite school of thought derives from a moderate Shiite sect which, unlike other Shiite sects, does not believe in the infallibility of Imam ʿAlī and does not vilify the Caliphs Abū Bakr and ʿUmar ibn al-Khaṭṭāb and the other Companions of the Prophet. The sect's origins are attributed to Zayd ibn ʿAlī Zayn al-Ābidīn (d. 122 AH/740 CE).

9.95